Advances in Theory and Practice of Emerging Markets

Series Editor

Yogesh K. Dwivedi
EMaRC, School of Management
Swansea University Bay Campus
Swansea, United Kingdom

Series Regional Editors

David Brown, Lancaster University, UK
Regions: China and UK

Lemuria Carter, Virginia Commonwealth University, USA
Region: North America

Marijn Janssen, TU Delft, The Netherlands
Region: Europe

Samuel Fosso Wamba, Toulouse Business School, France
Region: Africa

More information about this series at http://www.springer.com/series/15802

Sanjay Mohapatra • K. Ganesh
M. Punniyamoorthy • Rani Susmitha

Service Quality in Indian Hospitals

Perspectives from an Emerging Market

 Springer

Sanjay Mohapatra
Xavier Institute of Management
Bhubaneswar, India

M. Punniyamoorthy
Department of Management Studies
National Institute of Technology
Tiruchirappalli, Tamil Nadu, India

K. Ganesh
SCM Center of Competence
McKinsey & Company, Inc.
Chennai, Tamil Nadu, India

Rani Susmitha
Department of Management Studies
National Institute of Technology
Tiruchirappalli, Tamil Nadu, India

Advances in Theory and Practice of Emerging Markets
ISBN 978-3-319-88503-2   ISBN 978-3-319-67888-7   (eBook)
https://doi.org/10.1007/978-3-319-67888-7

Printed on acid-free paper

This Springer imprint is published by Springer Nature
The registered company is Springer International Publishing AG
The registered company address is: Gewerbestrasse 11, 6330 Cham, Switzerland

Abstract

The health-care industry is a wide and intensive form of services which are related to the well-being of human beings. The health-care industry covers hospitals, health insurances, medical software, health equipment and pharmacies. The Indian health-care industry is estimated to reach USD 155 billion in terms of revenues by 2017, according to a study by LSI Financial Services. Over the next 5 years, the size of the health-care industry is expected to almost double driven by the rise in per capita spending on health care, change in demographic profile, transition in disease profile, increase in health insurance penetration and fast-growing medical tourism market.

The rise and evolution of hospitals dates back to centuries; the hospital has emerged from curing providence to curing-cum-caring destiny. India is a country where a doctor is considered next to god in the context of the Sanskrit verse 'Vaidhyo Narayano Harihi'. In today's hospitals, the patient is all-important. The satisfaction of the patient is the route to success for the hospital. So, the emphasis should be given on patient satisfaction and service quality of the hospital. That idea provoked the interest for this study.

In this book, there are nine chapters elaborating regarding the work carried out.

Chapter 1 elaborates on the introduction to the hospital industry, evolution of hospitals, hospital departments, types of patients and patient satisfaction scenario in detail.

Chapter 2 deals with the literature review. The literature is divided into three stages. The first stage of literature speaks about the demographical studies in health care. The second stage of literature speaks about the SERVQUAL origin, modification and application. The third stage of literature deals with applications of data mining techniques like artificial neural networks (ANNs) and support vector machines (SVMs) in the health-care industry.

Chapter 3 gives us the issues related to the literature dealt with in Chap. 2. Based on the issues, objectives have been framed, and the scope of the research has been explained in this chapter.

Chapter 4 deals with the methodology applied in order to approach the objectives. In addition, the instrument considered for data collection and the procedure of data collection have been explained in detail. Justification of the model has been explained in this chapter.

Chapter 5 deals with the demographical indices like 'age' and 'gender', as well as clinical quality indicators like 'length of stay in hospital' and 'number of visits to the hospital'. This chapter also deals with the influence of demographical indices and clinical quality indicators on patient satisfaction.

Chapter 6 deals with causal model development. In this chapter, the influence of ten service quality dimensions on patient satisfaction has been determined by using structural equation modelling (SEM). Based on the path estimate scores, the dimensions have been ranked. Specialty cardiac care is taken as a benchmark. The difference in rankings between specialty cardiac care and multispecialty hospitals has been determined and explained.

Chapter 7 deals with artificial neural networks (ANNs). Here a classification model has been developed by using ANN. The factor scores obtained from the SEM model are taken as an input. The significance of the weights has been determined. Based on the weights, the contribution of the weights has been formulated and compared among specialty and multispecialty cardiac care hospitals. The model has been validated using confusion matrix.

Chapter 8 deals with support vector machines (SVMs). The factor scores obtained from the SEM model have been taken as an input. Nonlinear classifier equation has been used with radial basis function (RBF) in order to classify the patients. The model has been validated using confusion matrix. The apparent error rates of both ANN and SVM have been compared in order to find the best classification technique among the two.

Chapter 9 deals with the summary of the research and conclusion. The results have been discussed in detail at the end of each chapter. A brief summarization of the results has been given in the conclusion. In addition, the research implications and the scope for the future research have been discussed.

Keywords Service quality • Cardiac care hospitals • Demographics • Structural equation modelling • Artificial neural network • Support vector machines

Contents

Abbreviations

ANN   Artificial neural network
RBF   Radial basis function
SVM   Support vector machine
SEM   Structural equation model
STDs   Sexually transmitted diseases
SERVQUAL   Service quality

List of Figures

List of Tables

Chapter 1
Introduction

Contents

© Springer International Publishing AG 2018
S. Mohapatra et al., *Service Quality in Indian Hospitals*, Advances in Theory and
Practice of Emerging Markets, https://doi.org/10.1007/978-3-319-67888-7_1

1.1 Introduction

The service industry has always been a topic of interest to researchers due to its multifaceted nature and continuous evolution. In particular, health-care services attract researchers due to rapid growth in the current scenario. Health-care industry is a wide and intensive form of services which are related to the well-being of human beings. Health care is a social sector, and it operated at state level with the help of central government in India. Health-care industry covers hospitals, health insurances, medical software, health equipments and pharmacy. The Indian health-care industry is estimated to reach USD 155 billion in terms of revenues by 2017, according to a study by LSI Financial Services (Web link 1). Over the next 5 years, the size of the health-care industry is expected to almost double driven by rise in per capita spending on health care, change in demographic profile, transition in disease profile, increase in health insurance penetration and fast-growing medical tourism market. The major inputs of health-care industries are as listed below:

  I. Hospitals
 II. Medical insurance
III. Medical software
IV. Health equipments

1.2 Evolution of Hospitals: A Journey from Past to Present

A hospital is an institution for providing treatment to the patients with the help of specialized staff and equipment. Hospital incarnated in many forms like almshouse for the poor, hostel for pilgrims, hospital school, etc., before transforming into the present-day modern hospital. The etymology of the hospital roots from Latin '*hospes*' meaning 'host'. The word also is related to the Sanskrit word 'Ispital' and the German 'Spital'(Web link 2).

There is a proverb that 'History matters because it helps us not to repeat the mistakes'. So here are some of the early examples of hospital history.

In many of the ancient cultures, religion and medicine were interlinked. Egyptian temples were the earliest documented institutions aimed at providing cure. In ancient Greece, temples dedicated to the healer-god 'Asclepius', known as 'Asclepieia', functioned as centres of medical advice, prognosis and healing.

Even India has been reported to have institutions created specifically to care for the ill. 'King Asoka' is renowned to have built at least 18 hospitals (230 B.C.) with physicians and nursing staff. Stanley Finger (2001) in his book *Origins of Neuroscience: A History of explorations in to brain function* cites that 'Everywhere King Piyadasi (Asoka) erected two kinds of hospitals, hospitals for people and hospitals for animals' (Web link 3).

Persia is considered to be home for the first teaching hospital known as 'Academy of Gundishapur'. Here, the students were authorized to practise old medicine in presence of experts which paved a way for the development of medical education.

Every civilization and every empire contributed their role in the history of hospitals which are briefly described below.

1.2.1 Roman Empire

Around 100 B.C. 'valetudinarian', an institution to take care of sick slaves, gladiators and soldiers, was excavated in Roman Empire. The First Council of Nicaea of Roman Empire in 325 A.D. advised the church for the construction of a hospital for the poor, sick, widows and strangers in every cathedral town. It leaded to the expansion of hospitals all over the empire. The first hospitals were built by the physician Saint 'Sampson' in 'Constantinople' and by 'Basil', a bishop of Caesarea. The latter emerged hospitals were attached to a monastery and provided lodgings for poor, travellers, sick and lepers.

1.2.2 Medieval Persia and Islam

In the medieval Islamic world, the first hospital was built by 'Al-Walidibn Abdul Malik' (ruled 705–715 C.E.). In the medieval Islamic world, the word 'bimaristan' was used to indicate an establishment where the ills were welcomed and cared for by qualified staff. Muslim physicians were first to distinguish between a hospital and a hospice, asylum, lazaret or leper house, all of which were more concerned with isolating the sick and the mad from society than offering them a cure. So, the medieval 'bimaristan' hospitals were considered as 'the first hospitals' in the modern sense of the word.

The first hospital in Egypt was opened in 872 A.D., and thereafter public hospitals sprang up all over the empire from 'Spain' and the 'Maghrib' to Persia. As the system developed, physicians and surgeons were appointed who gave lectures to medical students and issued diplomas to those who were considered qualified to practise. The first psychiatric hospital was built in Baghdad in 705.A.D. Many other Islamic hospitals also had their own wards dedicated to mental health.

Between the eighth and twelfth centuries, Muslim hospitals developed a high standard of health care. Hospitals in Baghdad in the ninth and tenth centuries employed up to 25 staff physicians and had separate wards for different conditions. 'Al-Qairawan' hospital and mosque in Tunisia built under the 'Aghlabid' rule in 830 A.D. was simple but adequately equipped with halls organized into waiting rooms, a mosque and a special bath. The hospital employed female nurses, including nurses from Sudan. In addition to regular physicians who attended the sick, there were

'Fuqaha al-Badan', a kind of religious physiotherapists, group of religious scholars whose medical services included bloodletting, bone setting and cauterization.

1.2.3 Medieval Europe

An old French term for hospital 'hôtel-Dieu', which means 'hostel of God', is also considered as the preceding institution to the modern hospital. They were religious communities, with care provided by monks and nuns. Some were attached to monasteries; others were independent and had their own endowments, usually of property, which provided income for their support. Some hospitals were multifunctional, while others were founded for specific purposes such as leper hospitals or as refuges for the poor or for pilgrims: not all cared for the sick. 'Hospicio Cabañas' was the largest hospital in colonial America, in Guadalajara, Mexico.

The first Spanish hospital, founded by the Catholic bishop 'Masona' in 580 at Mérida, was a 'xenodochium' designed as an inn for travellers (mostly pilgrims to the shrine of Eulalia of Mérida) as well as a hospital for citizens and local farmers. The hospital's endowment consisted of farms to feed its patients and guests.

1.2.4 Colonial America

The first hospital founded in the America was the hospital 'San Nicolas de Bari' in Santo Domingo with an authorized construction from December 29, 1503 onwards. This hospital apparently incorporated a church. The first phase of its construction was completed in 1519, and it was rebuilt in 1552. Abandoned in the mid-eighteenth century, the hospital now lies in ruins near the Cathedral in Santo Domingo.

The first hospital north of Mexico was the 'Hôtel-Dieu de Québec'. It was established in New France in 1639 by three Augustinians from 'Hôtel-Dieu de Dieppe' in France.

1.2.5 Incredible India

India also contributes its part to the hospital history. The present 'Osmania Medical College' in Andhra Pradesh is the oldest medical school in India and perhaps Asia. The concept of Osmania Medical College dates back to 1595 A.D., then called as 'Dar-Ul-Shifa' in Hyderabad, making it the oldest medical school.

Osmania has a rich history of pioneering medical innovations. For the first time, *chloroform* was used as an anaesthetic in Osmania General Hospital. The causative agent of malaria was elucidated by 'Sir Ronald Ross' who has been immortalized by the 'Sir Ronald Ross Institute of Tropical and Communicable Diseases' (popular by name Fever Hospital) affiliated to Osmania.

The medium of instruction was initially Urdu and the degree awarded was 'Hakeem'. Later the medium is changed to English. Osmania Medical College is a medical school in Hyderabad, Andhra Pradesh, India. It was founded in 1846 as the *Hyderabad Medical School* making it one of the oldest medical schools in the world. It is presently affiliated to the NTR University of Health Sciences. The College was originally affiliated to the Osmania University of Hyderabad. It is the only medical college in India (and perhaps the world), where each medical specialty has a separate training hospital.

1.2.6 Modern Era

In Europe, the medieval concept of Christian care evolved during the sixteenth and seventeenth centuries into a secular one, but it was in the eighteenth century that the modern hospital began to appear, serving only medical needs and staffed with physicians and surgeons. The 'Charité' founded in Berlin in 1710 is an early example.

'Guy's Hospital' was founded in London in 1724 by the wealthy merchant, 'Thomas Guy'. Other hospitals sprang up in London and other British cities over the century, many paid for by private subscriptions. In the British American colonies, the Pennsylvania General Hospital was chartered in Philadelphia in 1751.

The Vienna General Hospital is the world's largest hospital; it opened in 1784. It gradually developed into the most important research centre. Basic medical science expanded and specialization advanced. Furthermore, the first dermatology, eye, as well as ear, nose and throat clinics in the world were founded in Vienna. So the place is being considered as the birth of specialized medicine.

By the mid-nineteenth century, most of Europe and the United States had established a variety of public and private hospital systems. In continental Europe, the new hospitals generally were built and run from public funds. The National Health Service (NHS), the principle provider of health care in the United Kingdom, was founded in 1948.

In the United States, the traditional hospital is a non-profit hospital, usually sponsored by a religious denomination. One of the earliest of these 'almshouses' was started by William Penn in Philadelphia in 1713. These hospitals are tax-exempt due to their charitable purpose but provide only a minimum of charitable medical care. They are supplemented by large public hospitals in major cities, and research hospitals often affiliated with a medical school. The largest public hospital system in America is the New York City Health and Hospitals Corporation, which includes 'Bellevue Hospital', the oldest US hospital, affiliated with New York University Medical School. In the late twentieth century, chains of for-profit hospitals arose in the United States.

Similarly the unleashed history of modern hospital dates back to the centuries. While churning it down, we can observe the magnificent evolution of the present-day modern hospital (Web link 4).

1.3 Types of Hospitals

There are different types of hospitals based on their specializations, number of beds or their activities. Broadly they are classified as follows:

1.3.1 General Hospitals

The best known type of hospital is the general hospital, which is set up to deal with many kinds of disease and injury, and typically has an emergency department to deal with immediate and urgent threats to health. A general hospital typically is the major health-care facility in its region, with large number of beds for intensive care and long-term care, along with specialized facilities for surgery, plastic surgery, childbirth, bioassay laboratories and so forth. Larger cities may have many several hospitals of varying sizes and facilities.

1.3.2 Specialty Hospitals

Types of specialized hospitals include hospitals concentrated on particular fraternity like neuro care, nephro care, cancer care, cardiac care, trauma centres, rehabilitation hospitals, children's hospitals, seniors' (geriatric) hospitals and hospitals for dealing with specific medical needs such as psychiatric problems, certain disease categories and so forth.

1.3.3 Super Speciality and Multispecialty Hospitals

These are the hospitals with more than one specialty or super speciality and are operated together to care and cure for maximum sorts of illness under a single roof. The number of beds here will be comparatively less than that of general hospitals but will be more than that of a specialty hospital.

1.3.4 Teaching Hospitals

A teaching hospital combines assistance to patients with teaching to medical students and nurses. It is often linked to a medical school or nursing school. Some of these are associated with universities.

1.3.5 Clinics

If a medical facility smaller than a hospital is generally called a clinic and is often run by a government agency for health services or a private partnership of physicians. Clinics generally provide only outpatient services (Web link 5).

The pictographic representation of the types of hospitals is shown in Fig. 1.1.

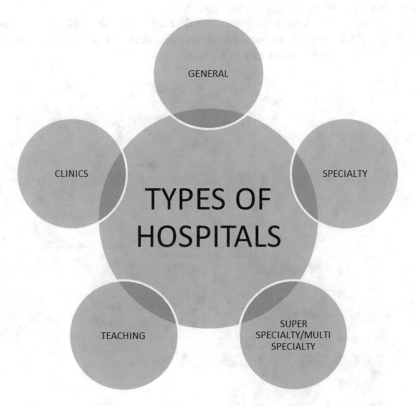

Fig. 1.1 Types of hospitals

1.4   Hospital Departments

Hospitals vary widely in the services they offer, and therefore there is a classification segment in the departments they have. They are classified briefly as intramural and extramural departments. Intramural are the departments existing within the hospital, and the extramural are the departments outside the hospital, nevertheless facilitating the hospital like blood bank, diagnostic labs, pharmacy, etc. The intramural department is further classified into clinical and administrative departments. Clinical departments are involved with the clinical services for the patients, whereas administrative departments are involved with the proper execution of hospital services and hospital administration. For example, the administrative departments are operations department, medical records department, etc.

The clinical departments are further classified as general and specialized departments. In general, they may have acute services such as an emergency department or specialist trauma centre. These may then be backed up by more specialist units such as cardiology, neurology, oncology, obstetrics, gynaecology, etc. The pictographic representation of it is shown in Fig. 1.2.

Some hospitals will have outpatient departments, and some will have chronic treatment units such as behavioural health services, dentistry, dermatology, psychiatric ward, rehabilitation services and physiotherapy.

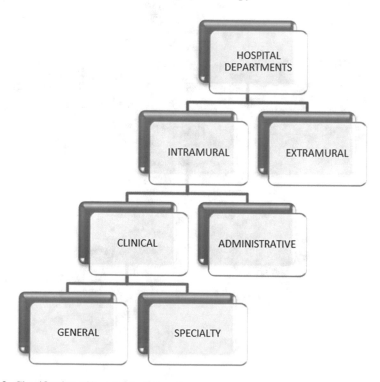

Fig. 1.2 Classification of hospital departments

1.5 Types of Patients

Some patients go to a hospital just for diagnosis, treatment or therapy and then leave, without staying overnight. They are considered as the 'outpatients'. Others are 'admitted' and stay overnight or for several weeks or months, and they are considered as the 'inpatients'.

1.6 Public and Private Sectors

According to National Family Health Survey-3, the private medical sector remains the primary source of health care for the majority of households in both urban areas (70%) and rural areas (63%) of India. Reliance on public and private health-care sector varies significantly between states. Several reasons are cited for relying on private rather than public sector; the topmost reason at national level is poor quality of care in public sector, with more than 57% households pointing to this as the reason for the preference of private health care. Other major reasons are distance of the public sector facility, long waiting time and inconvenient hours of operation (Web link 6).

1.7 Customer of a Hospital

A customer from the hospital perspective is any individual or institution who is an actual, potential or future user of the hospital and its various services. The customer from the hospital is very different from the regular customer, the difference being that he doesn't want to be a 'customer' in the first place.

The customer of a hospital is entirely different from the customers of other service industries, because unlike customers of other service sectors, their need for the service is not voluntary, and it is a decision imposed on him by his poor health and afflictions. The patient spends money unwillingly, and hospitals should be sensitive to this fact while dealing with them. Even a small deficiency can be a crucial factor in determining the patient's satisfaction and their eventual revisit to the same hospital. Service providers have to realize that satisfaction is the main factor for their survival. So, it will be very useful to know the specific dimensions which influence the patient satisfaction, for the better delivery of services of a hospital. The workings of the hospital are laid bare to the patient, and every interaction the patient has with any staff member is a crucial factor in determining whether he would choose the same hospital again.

1.8   Patient Satisfaction Scenario in Modern Hospitals

Customer satisfaction is a person's feeling of pleasure or disappointment resulting from comparing a product/service's perceived performance or outcome in relation to his or her expectations. As this definition makes clear, satisfaction is a function of perceived performance and expectations. If the performance falls short of expectations, the customer is dissatisfied. If the performance matches the expectations, the customer is satisfied. If the performance exceeds expectations, the customer is highly satisfied or delighted.

Therefore, on applying this concept to the hospital sector, 'Customer satisfaction in a hospital is basically a state of mind of the patient. It is the ability of your hospital service to meet the expectations of the patient. Customer delight is all about exceeding the expectations of the patients to make him highly satisfied with the hospital'. In today's hospital market, the patient is all-important. Therefore to achieve patient satisfaction, the hospital has to develop itself technologically, as well as become more service-oriented.

It is essential for a hospital to reach out to its customers (patients), if it wants to survive the competition. This can be achieved only by building a bridge of trust between the hospital and the community (Web link 7).

1.9   Why Cardiac Care?

Each hospital deals with many specialities among which 'cardiac care' is crucial due to its varied intricacies. Cardiac care is a hospital's biggest revenue earner (Web link 8). While considering specifically the patient satisfaction of cardiac patients, it is entirely a different picture. Cardiac patients have the innate fear of losing their life; they will be highly anxious about their treatment and will think that their doctor is their only rescuer. So, if the hospital solves their problems using proper medication, counselling sessions, successful operation and with empathetic treatment, they will be the highly satisfied and loyal customers to the hospitals and could play an important role in promoting the hospital through word of mouth.

As per the world heart foundation statistics (Web link 9), the mortality due to cardiovascular disease is becoming epidemic. Especially in the urban areas of India, the annual case load for cardiac surgery is between 70 and 80 thousand, of which more than 60% are coronary artery operations. The annual caseload has doubled since 1995. Hence, these statistics depict the importance of cardiac care in India.

1.10   Quality Cardiac Care Is the Need of the Hour

Here in India, which is well known as the land of ancient medicine, an idiom is most prevalent, i.e. 'doctor is next to god'. This is very well suited for the context of cardiac patients because they are highly satisfied comparatively, as their intense pain and fear will be relieved after treatment, and a highly responsive immediate care is available to them. The patients don't neglect medication as well, because it matters their life. Usually the recurrence period of the heart diseases is long, so contended patients coming for follow-ups will express their deep gratitude, and it will result in word of mouth publicity from the patient. So the studies of cardiac patients' satisfaction will be highly useful in the current situation, as they will help corporate hospitals to focus on the most important service quality criteria influencing the satisfaction of the patient.

Moreover India has become the hub for cardiac treatment in a fruitful way and is attracting many medical tourists every year (Web link 10). The affordable and quality care available here is the base for it. The Indian hospital literature reflects satisfaction studies in different aspects but till now no attempt has been made to compare the satisfaction of cardiac patients among specialized cardiac hospitals and multi-specialty hospitals having cardiac care as one of their specialities.

1.11   Motivation for the Research

With respect to all the stats highlighted above, it is clear that health care and hospital sector are booming. It is the time for research in the arena. As discussed, measurement of patients' satisfaction with services provided by the concerned hospital is important from two angles. Firstly, patients constitute the hospital's direct clients. Thus overall satisfaction of the patient is an important aspect of the service itself. Secondly, patient satisfaction provides an indirect measure of the other dimensions as well. So, recognizing the need for research on patient satisfaction and the dimensions affecting it, hospitals and health-care organizations are increasingly turning towards it, in order to continuously improve quality of service. This aroused the need for research in this domain.

After scrutinizing the facts about private cardiac care hospitals, which are mushrooming at a very rapid speed in order to attract customers, a proper patient satisfaction study in the same fraternity will be quite helpful. It provoked the interest for this research.

Studies aiming at the influence of service quality dimensions on satisfaction are the need of the hour in the current situation. Such studies will help the hospitals not only in verifying their mistakes in delivering service but also help in attracting new customers to the hospital.

Even though ample of approaches and studies existed on patient satisfaction, a study with staunch statistical back up is quite necessary for its practical implementation. So, all these factors motivated for undertaking the current research.

1.12   The Structure of the Book

This book is organized as follows:

In Chap. 1, we introduce the area of our research, namely, patient satisfaction studies among cardiac care hospitals.

The related works by other researchers in this area are compiled under the head literature survey in Chap. 2.

We then give the research gap, problem definition, scope and objective in Chap. 3.

In Chap. 4, we elaborate the research methodology adopted in developing the three models.

In Chap. 5, the influence of demographic variables has been studied.

In Chaps. 6, 7 and 8, we explain the development of three models, i.e. structural equation modelling, artificial neural networking and support vector machines, respectively, to determine the patient satisfaction.

The comparison of the result of the empirical study is reported, and the research is concluded in Chap. 9.

Thus, in this book we have formalized the definition of the problem, developed the models on data from the cardiac care hospitals and have presented our results.

1.13   Conclusion

This chapter depicts the picture of health-care industry in brief. The evolution of the hospitals, types of hospitals, departments in hospitals, etc. has been elucidated in this chapter. In addition to the nature of the hospital industry, role of patient satisfaction in the industry has been described in brief. Likewise the need for the research in the health-care domain has been highlighted in this chapter.

Chapter 2
Literature Review

Contents

2.1 Introduction

The literature review has been organized in three stages. The first stage is about the literature of the demographical indices, the second stage is about the literature on the SERVQUAL and the third stage is the literature about the data mining applications in service industries.

The first stage explains about the literature pertaining to the demographical indices and their impact in health-care industry. This literature helps to enlighten us about the importance of demographical indices in a health-care body like hospital.

The second stage is about the literature dealing with the whole SERVQUAL concept like its origin, modifications, applications to study the patient's satisfaction and comparison of public and private hospitals. This chapter speaks about the whole SERVQUAL concept of hospital industry in a nutshell.

The third stage is the application of the data mining techniques in the service industry to measure customer satisfaction, including health care. This elucidates the applicability of data mining techniques in the broad industry.

© Springer International Publishing AG 2018
S. Mohapatra et al., *Service Quality in Indian Hospitals*, Advances in Theory and
Practice of Emerging Markets, https://doi.org/10.1007/978-3-319-67888-7_2

2.2   First Stage: Literature on Demographics

The first stage of literature deals with the demographic variables and their effect in health-care scenario. By going through the literature, many studies of demographic variables in health-care industry have been examined, and they are discussed as follows:

Rosenthal et al. (1997) studied the influence of demographic variables on sexually transmitted diseases (STDs).The study proved that the factors like age and gender will affect the psychological condition of adolescents with STDs. The study revealed that, along with age and gender, the number of life partners and the attitude of an individual will play a pivotal role in the STD acquisition.

Wahl et al. (1999) studied the relation between clinical variables and demographic variables and also the aspects of quality of life on patients suffering from psoriasis. The study portrayed that the demographic and clinical variables combine to explain variance in health status, the perception of living with psoriasis and overall quality of life. While most of the variance is explained by the clinical variables, the disease-specific disability variable seems to be an important mediating factor in the study.

Schonall et al. studied the influence of both demographic and disease-related variables among cancer patients which are categorized as low-risk patients, moderate-risk patients and high-risk patients. In addition they clustered the factors which influenced all the three risk sets of patients.

Schwartz and Frohner (2005) studied the importance of the demographic variables among multiple sclerosis patients. The study also focussed on the study of quality of life inventory and expanded disability status to predict the mental health dimension of the patient groups using various questionnaires.

2.3   Second Stage: Literature on SERVQUAL

We have classified the literature review for service quality in hospital in a chronological order, and the same is represented in Fig. 2.1.

The picture depicts the literature survey of the origin of the 'SERVQUAL' concept, its modifications, its applications to study the patients' satisfaction and its comparison of public and private hospitals using SERVQUAL.

The first subdivision of the review deals with literature related to SERVQUAL origin. The scope and tremendous applications of service quality have been foreseen by Parasuraman et al. (1985). Initially they developed a service quality model which evolved through an exploratory survey consisting of five gaps related to customer and marketer. This guided to develop ten determinants in order to measure the perceived service quality. The ten determinants were further classified into three categories: (i) search properties [credibility and tangibles], (ii) credence properties [competence and security] and (iii) experience properties [reliability, responsiveness,

Fig. 2.1 Figure portraying the chronological order of substages in SERVQUAL literature

accessibility, courtesy, communication and understanding]. Later the ten determinants were debriefed into five dimensions in an increasing order of importance
which are reliability, assurance, tangibility, empathy and responsiveness, and these
are termed as a RATER scale (Parasuraman et al. 1988). The 97-item instrument has
been abridged to 22-item instrument leading to the development of SERVQUAL
instrument based on the highest factor loading scores.

Buttle (1996), in a SERVQUAL review article, stated a limitation of SEVQUAL,
stating that the five dimensions of SERVQUAL scale is not having a maximum variance. He also stated that, regardless of the limitations in SERVQUAL scale, it is still
one of the most extensively utilized measures of service quality. Since then, the
modification studies based on SERVQUAL were carried out immensely.

The second subdivision depicts the review of articles emulated as a modified
instrument from SERVQUAL instrument in health care.

Dabholkar et al. (1996) proposed varied dimensions for retail industry as retail
service quality scale. The five dimensions of the modified service quality scale are
'physical aspects (appearance, convenience), reliability (promises, doing it right),
personal interaction (inspiring confidence, courteous/helpful), problem solving and
policy'.

Bahia and Nantel (2000) have developed a banking service quality (BSQ) scale
with six dimensions, namely, 'effectiveness and assurance, access, price, tangibles,
services portfolio, reliability' by modifying the SERVQUAL scale with 31
variables.

Dean (1999) modified the SERVQUAL scale and identified four dimensions
which are stable. The dimensions used by them are 'assurance, tangibles, empathy

and reliability and responsiveness'. Here, the fourth dimension is a fusion of two dimensions. They compared the service quality dimensions in different health-care settings like medical centre and maternal and child health centres.

Kilbourne et al. (2004) modified the SERVQUAL scale into four-dimensional modified scale including 'tangibles, responsiveness, reliability and empathy'. They studied the overall satisfaction of patients from various hospitals of the United States and United Kingdom. Even many studies modified the SERVQUAL scale which can be applicable precisely to hospitals.

Arasli et al. (2008) developed a six-dimensional SERVQUAL instrument with the dimensions 'empathy, giving priority to the inpatient needs, relationship between staff and patients, professionalism of staff, food and physical environment'. The expectation, the perception and the gap scores of patient satisfaction were evaluated for the hospitals of Cyprus island. The results proved that the health-care services were better in private hospitals.

Fowdar study categorically says that the SERVQUAL instrument should be changed based on its applications. He developed a new patient satisfaction instrument 'PRIVHEALTHQUAL' by adding two new factors 'fair and equitable treatment' and 'equipment and records'; they validated their study at private hospitals.

Ariffin and Aziz (2008) applied SERVQUAL instrument in hospitals and developed a new scale called 'HOSPIQUAL'. Here only four of the SERVQUAL dimensions were considered. The instrument has the provision to find out the 'zone of tolerance' for desired versus adequate services. They applied this to find the gap scores of patient's expected and perceived satisfaction in hospitals through gap analysis.

Aagja and Garg (2010) developed a new scale 'PubHosQual' for measuring perceived service quality for public hospitals from the patient's perspective. SERVQUAL model is generic in nature, and it has been modified according to the requirements of public hospitals with the five dimensions, namely, 'admission, medical service, overall service, discharge process and social responsibility'.

By considering the modification studies and comparing them with SERVQUAL scale, there are some differences among the dimensions which the researchers have used, and they are highlighted here at a glance. In the studies of Dabholkar et al. (1996), only reliability dimension is considered from SERVQUAL scale; remaining dimensions have been modified in retail service quality. When considering Bahia and Nantel (2000) studies, dimensions like tangibles and reliability were considered as same, but remaining dimensions have been modified in banking service quality. In the studies of Dean (1999), the reliability and the responsiveness dimensions are merged into a single dimension, and the four dimensions considered for their studies were 'assurance, tangibles, empathy and reliability and responsiveness'. Kilbourne et al. (2004) also considered four dimensions from the SERVQUAL scale. Here the dimension 'assurance' has been omitted, and the other four dimensions were considered from the SERVQUAL scale. Fowdar (2008) in their studies considered the two more dimensions apart from the five dimensions of SERVQUAL. Ariffin and Aziz (2008) used only four dimensions by omitting the 'assurance' dimension from SERVQUAL scale. Aagja and Garg (2010) used five entirely new dimensions for 'PubHosQual' scale. From this we have found out that the dimensions like reliability and tangibility are just carried on, but there are several new alterations and modifications which are carried out on other dimensions.

The third subdivision deals with application of SERVQUAL in hospitals and patient satisfaction studies. Babakus and Mangold (1992) brought out the usefulness of SERVQUAL by analysing its consistencies for back stage (administration and non-administration employees) of hospital and front stage (consumers) of hospital to assess expectations and perceptions of service quality for the improvement of satisfaction levels.

Eric Reidenbach and Smallwood (1990) studied the impact of ten service quality dimensions on overall patient's service perception, satisfaction with the treatment they received and their willingness to recommend the hospital to others. They used all the ten determinants of service quality and further abridged the sub-criteria of the ten factors into seven factors based on their valid factor loading scores. They also assessed patient confidence among inpatients, outpatients and emergency patients in their study.

Vandamme and Leunis (1993) study was mainly on the SERVQUAL scale purification and its application to measure hospital service quality. They also tested the consistency of the scale through expectation, perception and difference scores.

Youssef et al. (1995) used SERVQUAL to measure the satisfaction levels of patients of multispecialty like orthopaedic care, spinal care, dental care, etc. at NHS in UK hospitals.

Simon S. K. Lam (1997) studied the patient's perceived service quality by implementing SERVQUAL in Hong Kong hospitals. This study asserts that the SERVQUAL instrument is more apt to measure service quality in health-care industry. He also analysed the validity, reliability and predictive validity of SERVQUAL and its applicability in health-care sector.

Baxter (2004) used SERVQUAL instrument for occupational health (OH) clients of Nottingham hospitals to know the satisfaction levels of the patients. This study proved that the reliability and assurance dimensions were given the top priority followed by responsiveness and empathy.

Jabnoun and Rasasi (2005) in their study administered two questionnaires to measure the SERVQUAL dimensions and to assess the relation between transactional leadership and service quality in UAE hospitals. They found that transformational leadership was positively associated with all the dimensions of the service quality.

Pakdil and Harwood (2005) used SERVQUAL instrument to analyse the patient's satisfaction with the gap scores of patient's expectation and perception. It was done to assess the patient satisfaction levels in a preoperative assessment clinic.

Mik and Hazel Wisniewski (2005) used SERVQUAL to study the satisfaction of patients in a colonoscopy unit. This study focussed on specific improvements for colonoscopy units, which were considered necessary in the patient's perception.

Rohini and Mahadevappa (2006) carried out studies about the service quality perception in hospitals of Bangalore, India, with the SERVQUAL questionnaire for the measurement of Gap 5 (patient perception and patient expectation) and Gap 1 (patient perception and management perception with respect to patient's expectation). This study concluded that the consistency between expectation and perception could be ensured either by bringing changes in professional behaviour and expectation or by altering patient's expectation and perception.

Wicks and Chin (2008) developed an overall satisfaction model by linking service process experience factors like preprocess service, processing service and postprocess service. As an extension, they added factors like belief and intention and developed a structural model. The study effectively evaluates the relationship between the overall satisfaction, loyalty and patient retention.

Elleuch (2008) studied the outpatient's satisfaction in Japanese hospitals using SERVQUAL instrument. This study identified two factors 'process characteristics' and 'physical appearance'. The study used a structural equation modelling by interlinking these factors along with overall satisfaction and intentional behaviours.

Chowdhury (2008) studied the health-care scenario of the Bangladesh hospitals using SERVQUAL scale. Mean scores of customer perceptions and expectations were compared between public and private hospitals. This study reflects some socio-economic factors like income, education and profession of the people which affect choosing the health-care quality. They haven't validated the results with statistical tools. But the study suggested some strategies to narrow the service quality gap and some policy recommendations to overcome the overall problems pertaining to Bangladesh health-care scenario.

Yaacob et al. (2011) applied SERVQUAL in Malaysian hospitals to know about the relationship between tangibility and responsiveness in influencing patient satisfaction. This study was conducted on the outpatients of the hospital.

Jager and Plooy (2011) conducted a study on inpatients and outpatients of public hospitals in South Africa. The expectation, perception and gap score of the two service quality dimensions reliability and tangibility were studied as the authors aimed on the literature which portrays that these two dimensions play a major role in determining the service quality.

The fourth subdivision deals with the comparison of public and private hospitals using SERVQUAL.

Mostafa (2005) applied SERVQUAL in hospitals to investigate how patients perceive service quality in Egypt's public and private hospitals. In this paper the five dimensions of SERVQUAL were reduced to three dimensions. A discriminate function was developed to categorize patients who selected public hospitals and those who selected private hospitals.

Taner and Antony (2006) study speaks on five dimensions of SERVQUAL instrument. The article measures the comparison of patient satisfaction levels in private and public hospitals in Turkey. The perception, expectation and the gap scores were measured, and the results showed that the private hospitals were comparatively good in service quality. They haven't validated the results with statistical tools.

Owusu-Frimpong and Nwankwo (2010) conducted a study on patient satisfaction comparing both general and corporate hospitals on their performances in terms of patient satisfaction. Their study concluded that a corporate hospital patient's satisfaction is comparatively higher than that of a general hospital patient's satisfaction.

Alrubaiee and Alkaaida (2011) conducted a study on public and private hospitals to know the relationship between patient perceptions of health-care quality and patient satisfaction. This study also portrayed the patient trust as the mediating effect of patient satisfaction. The study also showed that the significance of socio-demographic variables affects patient's satisfaction.

2.4   Third Stage: Literature on Data Mining Techniques

The literature related to data mining is reviewed in this chapter and is framed as follows:

As pertaining to tourism industry, the data mining techniques have been used for mass customization and to reduce the costs of travelling by Bashar Al-Salim (2008). The study aims at minimizing the operation and processing costs for the service provider and to maximize customer satisfaction on the other.

Golmohammadi et al. (2011) used neural networks to predict the overall satisfaction of the tourists; the study has been carried out in Iran. The study found that 'improving tourism infrastructures of the country' in addition to 'globally promoting the image of Iran' is of the highest priority for Iran's tourism industry to reach to its full potential.

In the health-care industry, data mining tools were used in health insurance information system by Marisa Viveros et al. (1996). Neural networking was used to detect the profitable customers for dental clinics at Taiwan by Wan-I-Lee and Shih (2007). Neural networks were in turn used for fraud detection in health-care industry by Jing Li et al. (2007). The usage of neural networks is not limited to hospital management; it has its extension and applications on the clinical side also.

Khasman (2008) in his paper aimed to classify the blood cells accurately and efficiently in least possible time based on its morphological features using neural networks. This was done through feature extraction phase and identification phase. Back propagation algorithm was used in the study; the pixel readings of the images were taken as the input for training and testing the data. The neural network proved to be 99.17% accurate in classifying the blood cells.

Alanis et al. (2011) conducted their study on type 1 diabetes mellitus patients. Recurrent multilayer perceptron method was used with Kalman filtering algorithm. Modelling of blood glucose levels was tested on a male and a female with continuous glucose monitoring. In addition the time series analysis was used and the study predicted the blood glucose levels.

Because of the gradual development of data mining techniques, even the clinical arena of health-care industry focussed on it. Ping Hsu et al. (2010) carried out a work on neonatal babies at Taiwan hospitals. The practice of newborn screening is carried out to prevent permanent disabilities and that screening system is developed using support vector machine (SVM) classifications. This is carried out by considering the data from mass spectrometry which is used to interpret and determine whether a newborn has a metabolic disorder.

Patil et al. (2011) compared different data mining techniques like SVM, ANN (artificial neural networks), decision tree, etc. The study was carried out on burn patients from one of the Asia's largest hospital, situated in India. They predicted the survivability of burn patients using various data mining techniques. The performance comparison results have shown that the SVM technique is more accurate (96.12%) than back propagation of ANN (95%).

Ton Su et al. (2012) conducted studies on the patients suffering with ulcer caused due to pressure. They used the data mining techniques to predict the incidence of pressure ulcers. The results obtained showed that the data mining techniques are efficient in predicting the incidence of pressure ulcer.

2.5 Conclusion

This chapter articulates about the literature pertaining especially to the health-care domain. The review of the literature has been divided into three stages portraying the importance of demographic indices in hospital industry, service quality in hospital industry and usage of data mining techniques in hospital industry, respectively, in Sects. 2.2, 2.3 and 2.4. The issues based on these chapters will be discussed, and based on that, the objectives will be framed for the study in Chap. 3.

Chapter 3
Research Gap, Objectives and Scope

Contents

3.1 Introduction

From Chap. 2 it is evidenced that the piled up literature has some issues resulting in research gaps. So, the issues which require further study are identified from the literature, and the scope of research is elaborated. Based on these identified issues, the objectives have been framed for the research.

3.2 Research Gaps

The following issues have been left unanswered in the discussed literature. The issues are elaborated below:

© Springer International Publishing AG 2018   21
S. Mohapatra et al., *Service Quality in Indian Hospitals*, Advances in Theory and
Practice of Emerging Markets, https://doi.org/10.1007/978-3-319-67888-7_3

3.2.1   Issue 1

The demographical studies were carried out on various demographical factors like age, gender, ethnicity, place, etc., with respect to the diseases like STDs (sexually transmitted diseases), psoriasis, cancer, multiple sclerosis, etc. From the literature review, it is evident that no attempt has been made in analysing the impact of demographic variables on cardiac care.

3.2.2   Issue 2

From the literature review chapter, we could also convey that the Parasuraman's (1985) ten dimensions of service quality factors have been converged to five dimensions with 22 indicators forming SERVQUAL scale (tangibles, reliability, responsiveness, assurance and empathy). But in a distinctive service industry like the hospital industry, one needs more indicators representing the ten dimensions to measure the service quality. Especially the converged dimensions like accessibility, understanding, credibility, security, competence communication and courtesy play a key role in determining patient satisfaction in the hospital scenario. This is evidenced from the studies of Eric Reidenbach and Smallwood (1992) who used 41 indicators representing all the ten dimensions of service quality proposed by Parasuraman et al. (1985). Since then, there haven't been any definite studies in this perspective.

3.2.3   Issue 3

Till date, as per the available literature, comparative studies of specialty hospitals and general hospitals have been carried. But, no literature has covered details regarding the comparison of specialty and multispecialty hospitals.

3.2.4   Issue 4

By going through the customer satisfaction literature, many researchers have used data mining techniques to estimate satisfaction of the customers, Mohamed Mostafa (2009) in banking industry and Mei-Yu Wang (2007) in e-CRM (customer relationship management). Scant attention is provided in terms of using data mining techniques to classify the patient's satisfaction with health care.

3.3 Objectives of the Study

Based on the issues identified, the objectives for this research can be framed as follows:

1. To identify the influence of demographic variables and clinical quality variables on both specialty cardiac care and multispecialty hospitals
2. To develop a causal model for determining the order of importance of the dimensions that influence patient satisfaction using SEM (structural equation modelling)
3. To develop a classification model for classifying the patient satisfaction using ANN (artificial neural networking)
4. To develop a classification model for classifying the patient satisfaction using SVM (support vector machines), validating and comparing the classification models using confusion matrices

These objectives can unveil the solutions for the issues discussed in Sect. 3.2.

3.4 Scope of the Research

As there are no definite studies of all the ten dimensions of service quality after Eric Reidenbach et al., it ignites work with all the ten dimensions of service quality addressed by Parasuraman et al. and also to compare the patient satisfaction of speciality cardiac care and multispecialty hospitals. The classification model is needed in the hospital industry in order to classify the satisfaction of the patients and also to foresee the criteria to be taken care in order to satisfy a patient. Data mining techniques have revolutionized the performance measures in many areas; such a step is attempted in the health-care industry with this study. In addition a comparative study using two classifying models can be carried out to compare the output of the models in order to identify the best classification technique between the two.

The scope of the research is to identify the trait of cardiac hospitals (specialty or multispecialty) efficient in treating cardiac patients. The order of importance of service quality dimensions of much valued trait of the hospitals is determined to set as a benchmark. The classification of the cardiac patients is carried out by using two data mining techniques in order to identify an effective tool for classifying the patient, such that the dissatisfaction of the patient can be tracked resulting in a potential predictive tool for improving hospital performance.

3.5 Conclusion

In this chapter the issues were discussed which were extracted from the scrutiny of the literature review in Chap. 2. These issues were dwelling upon lack of proper demographical studies in cardiac care area, scant studies on ten service quality dimensions of Parasuraman et al. and comparative studies of specialty and multi-specialty hospitals and usage of data mining techniques in health care. Based on the identified issues, the objectives have been framed for the study. In addition the research scope of the study has been discussed in this chapter.

Chapter 4
Methodology

Contents

4.1 Introduction

This chapter gives us an understanding of how the data has been collected and used for our study. It provides a brief overview of each of the three techniques for the model considered in measuring patient satisfaction. The three techniques used in this context are structural equational modelling, artificial neural network and support vector machines.

© Springer International Publishing AG 2018
S. Mohapatra et al., *Service Quality in Indian Hospitals*, Advances in Theory and Practice of Emerging Markets, https://doi.org/10.1007/978-3-319-67888-7_4

We apply the data collected from the cardiac care hospitals across India to the three recognized techniques with reference to the model developed.

The procedure of collecting data has been explained as below:

4.2 Data Collection

The data is collected from 38 cardiac hospitals, which are listed by the Indian central government health scheme rules. The rules listed about 154 hospitals; 25% of the listed hospitals are offering cardiac services in India. The data collection is carried out in both the specialty (10) and multispecialty (28) hospitals from patients suffering with heart diseases. The data is obtained from the primary survey of the patients rating their satisfaction and the service quality factors influencing patient's satisfaction.

4.3 Sampling Design

The sampling design includes the sampling unit, the sample population, the sampling method used and the sample size determined. The sampling procedure adopted in this study is as given below:

4.3.1 Sampling Unit

The sampling unit is an element or a unit containing the element that is available for selection at some stage of the sampling process. The sampling unit consists of patients from cardiac care hospitals across India.

4.3.2 Sampling Frame

The sampling frame is usually a practical listing of the population or a definition of the elements which can be used for the sampling exercises.

The study considered the hospitals which are listed by the Indian central government health scheme rules. The rules listed about 154 hospitals; 25% of the listed hospitals, i.e. 38 hospitals, are offering cardiac services in India. So, the cardiac patients of these hospitals are considered as the sampling frame.

4.3.3   Sampling Method

The simple random sampling has been adopted in this study. Simple random sampling technique is a probability sampling technique in which each element in the population has a known and equal probability of selection. Every element is selected independent of other element, and the sample is drawn from the sampling frame. In the collection of data, randomness has been ensured by generating random numbers, and the patient has been selected by the corresponding IP (inpatient) numbers of inpatients from different hospitals.

4.3.4   Sample Size

In our study, a sample size of 705 numbers has been selected. The justification for the sample size is as follows: to run a LISREL model, one should have at least 13 times of the number of indicators. In this study, the number of indicators used to determine the patient satisfaction is 41. So, the sample size is $(13 \times 41 = 533)$ 533 as calculated. But excess of data is collected as a prior precaution because the data obtained is confidential, and it will be hectic to redo the data collection procedure again due to wide distribution of the sample collection points and sheer number of people involved and administrative concerns of the hospital.

4.3.5   Scale Used in Data Collection

This study used the validated questionnaire and collected responses on a 7-point Likert scale (ranging from 7, highly satisfied, to 1, highly dissatisfied). Three hundred patients of speciality cardiac care hospitals and 405 patients of multispecialty hospitals have provided data for the study. The data is used for testing the hypobook and to meet the objective of deriving the order of preference of the dimensions influencing the satisfaction of cardiac patients in the context provided.

4.4   Research Instrument

The instrument for this study is considered from the studies of Eric Reidenbach and Smallwood (1990), which has been validated by them. So, a pre-validated questionnaire consisting of 4 open-ended questions representing the demographic and clinical quality variables along with 41 indicators representing all the 10 dimensions is taken as an instrument to carry out the study. The responses were recorded in 7-point Likert scale. It is shown in Appendix 1. Table 4.1 depicts the total data collected.

Table 4.1 Table showing the data details from specialty cardiac care and multispecialty hospitals

	Specialty	Multispecialty	Total
Male	164	268	432
Female	136	137	273
Total	300	405	705

4.5 Model Justification

Parasuraman et al. (1985) have given perceived service quality model in which the ten dimensions, *accessibility, communication, competence, courtesy, credibility, reliability, responsiveness, security, tangibility and understanding*, influence the perceived service quality. It is represented in Fig. 4.1.

Nattakarn Earuku and Nik Kamariah Nik Mat (2008) have given a model in which perceived quality will be positively related to customer satisfaction. It is shown in Fig. 4.2

From the culmination of both models, we can justify that the ten dimensions will be influencing customer satisfaction. Here in this context of hospitals, it is patient satisfaction. So, the model developed is shown in Fig. 4.3.

In the developed model, the ten dimensions will be directly influencing the patient satisfaction as we understand that perceived service quality is positively related to customer satisfaction. A causal model is required to analyse and study the model. So, structural equation modelling (SEM) is used. Hence, the study justifies the new model development, in which all the ten dimensions of service quality will have a direct influence on patient's satisfaction and are used in this study to determine the satisfaction of cardiac patients

4.6 Objective 1: Demographic and Clinical Variables

As per the issues identified, the first objective framed is 'to identify the influence of demographical variables and clinical variables on both specialty and multispecialty cardiac care hospitals'. The clinical quality factors considered for the study are average length of stay and the number of visits to the hospital. The demographical factors considered for this study are gender and age. This has been elaborated and explained in detail in Chap. 5. Here, the influence of demographic variables on patient satisfaction is found out by using 'Z' test.

4.6.1 'Z' Test

A Z test is any statistical test for which the distribution of the test statistic under the null hypobook can be approximated by a normal distribution. Z test is carried out for both the specialty cardiac care hospitals and multispecialty cardiac care

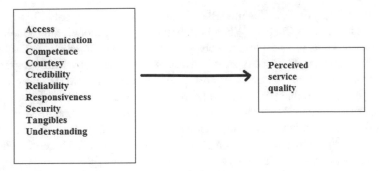

Fig. 4.1 Picture showing the relation of ten service quality dimensions on perceived service quality

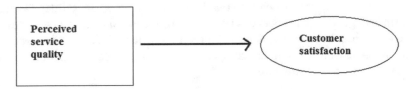

Fig. 4.2 Picture showing the relation of perceived service quality on customer satisfaction

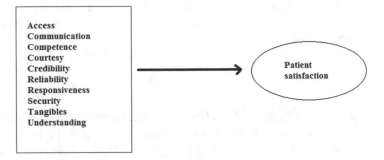

Fig. 4.3 Picture showing the influence of ten service quality dimensions on patient satisfaction

hospitals, and the results are compared for the interpretations. Thus Z test is carried out to find the significance of clinical quality indicators on patient's satisfaction.

4.7   Objective 2: Developing a Causal Model Using SEM

For the second objective, i.e. 'To develop a causal model for determining the order of importance of the dimensions, that influence patient satisfaction using SEM (Structural Equational Modelling)', the data collected is given as an input. Since SEM is a confirmatory technique, the model must be specified correctly based on the type of analysis that the modeller is attempting to confirm. This has been explained in detail in Chap. 6. When building the correct model, the modeller uses two different kinds of variables, namely, exogenous and endogenous variables. The distinction between these two types of variables is whether the variable regresses on another variable or not. As in regression, the dependent variable (DV) regresses on the independent variable (IV). In SEM terminology, other variables regress on exogenous variables. Exogenous variables can be recognized in a graphical version of the model, as the variables send out arrowheads, denoting which variable it is predicting. A variable that regresses on a variable is always an endogenous variable, even if this same variable is also used as a variable to be regressed on. Endogenous variables are recognized as the receivers of an arrowhead in the model. It is important to note that SEM is more general than regression. In particular a variable can act as both independent and dependent variable. Two main components distinguished in SEM are the *structural model* showing potential causal dependencies between endogenous and exogenous variables and the *measurement model* showing the relations between latent variables and their indicators. We can write a series of equations/statements that summarizes its configuration. As such, the summarization of measurement model structure is:

$$Y = \lambda_y \eta + \varepsilon \tag{4.1}$$

where 'λ' is the measurement model factor loading between the service quality dimensions and the indicators, 'ε' is measurement error terms and 'Y' observed variables, namely, indicators.

The summarization of structural model is as shown below:

$$\eta = \Gamma \xi + \zeta \tag{4.2}$$

where 'Γ' is structural factor loadings between service quality dimensions and cardiac patient's satisfaction, ζ is residual measurement error terms, η is the service quality dimension and ξ is the cardiac patient satisfaction. The service quality dimension with total satisfaction constitutes the structural model.

4.7.1 Test of Significance for Service Quality Factors

In the present context, we should find whether there is any overlap among the service quality dimensions. So, Barlett's test is used for the purpose. For this, the covariance matrix obtained from the output of SEM is considered, and the test is conducted to either accept or reject the null hypobook. The null hypobook for the test is:

H_0: The contribution of some factors is insignificant to the total variation of patient satisfaction.

Barlett's test is used to test the significance. Here the covariance matrix is considered as 's', and its testing is shown chronologically. Here, the matrix 's' is 10×10 matrix of all the service quality dimensions. The *Bartlett* approximate χ^2 value for the above covariance matrix 's' is given below:

$$\chi^2 = M \left[-\ln|S| + \sum_{j=1}^{k} \ln l_{(j)} + q \ln l \right]$$

In the p variable matrix, $p-k$ eigenvalues have nearly zero or zero values, then we should see whether it is better to retain k' components. $l_{(j)} = j$th eigenvalue from S. Then the q, m and 'l' are given as:

$$q = p - k$$

$$M = n - k - \frac{1}{6}\left(2q + 1 + 2/q\right)$$

$$l = \frac{1}{q}\left(tr(S) - \sum_{j=1}^{k} l_{(j)} \right)$$

The degrees of freedom are ½ $(p - k - 1)$ $(p - k + 2)$.

The same testing is carried out for multispecialty hospital also in order to test the significance of service quality factors.

4.8   Objective 3: Developing a Classification Model Using ANN

For the third objective, i.e. 'to develop a classification model for classifying the patient satisfaction using ANN (Artificial Neural Networks)', a classification model using an artificial neural network has been developed. It is explained in detail in Chap. 7. Here, the two neural network models (i) for speciality cardiac care hospitals and (ii) for multispecialty hospitals are developed for determining cardiac patient satisfaction. Input, hidden and output layers are the three layers of a neural network. Neurons are the computational units of the layer. The input neurons are the number of input variables. The data should be given as input in order to train and test the model. The latent variable score obtained from causal model for individual factors of service quality dimensions becomes the input data. The computed latent patient satisfaction factor score becomes the output value for the corresponding input values.

The number of hidden neurons was calculated based on the empirical formula given by Ying Wang and Huang (2009).

$$m = n + 0.618 \times (n-1)$$

where m is the number of hidden neurons and n is the number of input layer neurons. Here n is 10. The study considers the latent factor score as the cardiac patient satisfaction score based on the service quality dimensions. In this model the threshold value for the patient satisfaction is '0' and ranges from -1 to $+1$. If a patient scores more than threshold value, i.e. 0, he is a satisfied patient, and if he scores less than 0, then he is a dissatisfied patient. The magnitude of the satisfaction score tells us whether the patient is highly satisfied or not.

4.9   Objective 4: Developing a Classification Model Using SVM

For the fourth objective, 'to develop a classification model for classifying the patient satisfaction using SVM (Support Vector Machines) and validating and comparing the classification models using confusion matrices', the SVMs were adopted to predict the cardiac patient satisfaction. This has been dealt in detail in Chap. 8. SVMs can be broadly classified into three types, namely:

(a) Linearly separable classifier
(b) Linear soft margin classifier
(c) Nonlinear classifier

   SVM can be defined as a method for creation of an optimal hyperplane in a multidimensional space such that the hyperplane separates the two categories and has the lowest possible misclassification error. The hyperplane has the lowest misclassification error when it has the largest possible margin. Such a hyperplane can be called the maximum-margin hyperplane (Burges 1998). In this context, SVMs are used to classify a cardiac patient as 'satisfied' or 'dissatisfied', based on the learning algorithms ability to be trained on complex patterns and characteristics of interest that define magnitude of satisfaction in the training set and recognize similar patterns in the observed variables of the patients' satisfaction under investigation.

4.9.1   Validating and Comparing the Classification Models Using Confusion Matrices

For comparing the prediction accuracies and quantifying the error, we will go for confusion matrix or misclassification table. It provides us with a visual representation on the classification efficiency of the data mining techniques in classifying the data. It provides a grid where each row represents the predicted outcome and the columns represent the actual outcome. The numbers in the cells represent the actual

Table 4.2 Table depicting the framework of a confusion matrix

Confusion matrix		Predicted		
		Satisfied	Dissatisfied	Total
Actual	Satisfied	X_1	X_2	$\sum X = X_1 + X_2$
	Dissatisfied	Y_2	Y_1	$\sum Y = Y_1 + Y_2$
	Total	$X_1 + Y_2$	$X_2 + Y_1$	$\sum X + \sum Y$

number of true positives, false positives, false negatives and true negatives in the result of the classification obtained by using the SVM or ANN. Based on the values obtained, we can observe the most efficient model for classifying the data. It is depicted in Table 4.2.

The entries in the confusion matrix above are explained below in the context of our study:

- X_1 is the count of correct predictions that a patient belongs to 'Group Satisfied'.
- X_2 is the count of incorrect predictions that a patient belongs to 'Group Dissatisfied'.
- Y_2 is the count of incorrect predictions that a patient belongs to 'Group Dissatisfied'.
- Y_1 is the count of correct predictions that a patient belongs to 'Group Satisfied'.

4.10 Conclusion

This chapter explicates the approach of data collection, model development and the research tools to be used in the study to analyse the data. The general idea of the techniques used to analyse the framed objectives has been portrayed in this chapter.

A brief outline about the analysis of demographical indices, structural equational modelling, artificial neural networking and support vector machines has been discussed. The essence of the methodology rendered in this chapter is elaborated and has been equipped into individual chapters as the book continues.

Chapter 5
Analysis of Demographical Indices

Contents

5.1 Introduction

Demographics are the quantifiable statistics of a given population. Demographics are also used to identify the study of quantifiable subsets within a given population which characterize that population at a specific point in time. Demographical indices play a major role in every survey method of data collection procedure. They give us the basic yet broad segmentation of the data. The demographical indices used in this study are gender and age. The overall demographical classification indices are depicted in Tables 5.1.

The data is portrayed and analysed individually for specialty cardiac care hospitals and for multispecialty hospitals.

© Springer International Publishing AG 2018
S. Mohapatra et al., *Service Quality in Indian Hospitals*, Advances in Theory and
Practice of Emerging Markets, https://doi.org/10.1007/978-3-319-67888-7_5

Table 5.1 Table showing the demographical details of specialty and multispecialty cardiac care hospitals

Demographic variable	Range	Specialty cardiac care Frequency		Multispecialty cardiac care Frequency	
		Male	Female	Male	Female
Age	20–30	15	4	4	4
	30–40	67	21	49	46
	40–50	44	49	93	51
	50–60	30	26	113	16
	60–70	8	36	9	20

5.2 Demographics of Specialty Cardiac Care Hospitals

The analysis of data for specialized cardiac care hospitals is as follows:

The specialized hospitals consist a total of 300 data patient's data which constitutes 164 (54%) male and 136 (46%) female respondents. The demographical factors considered here are age and gender.

5.2.1 Age

The age ranges from 20 to 70 years. The highest frequency of people prone to heart diseases in male is in the age group of 30–40 years constituting 41% of males, followed by the age group of 40–50 years constituting 27% of males, whereas in females, 40–50 years is the age group which is more prone to heart diseases with 36% followed by 50–60 years of age group with a susceptibility of 20%.

5.3 Demographics of Multispecialty Cardiac Care Hospitals

The data of multispecialty hospitals consists of 405 respondents with 268 (66%) males and 137 (34%) females. Gender and age were considered as demographical factors.

5.3.1 Age

Here the highest frequency of people prone to heart diseases among males is in the age group of 50–60 years constituting 42% of males, followed by the age group of 40–50 years constituting 35% of males, whereas in females, 40–50 years is the age group which is more prone to heart diseases with 37% of the surveyed group, followed by 30–40 years of age group with a susceptibility of 34%. It is depicted in Fig. 5.1.

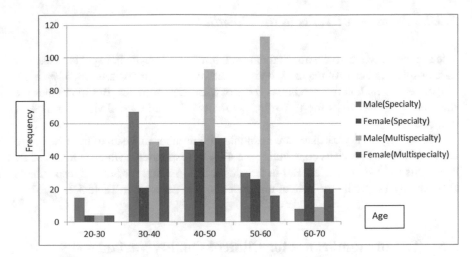

Fig. 5.1 Graph representing the age factor of both specialty and multispecialty cardiac care hospital with *x*-axis representing age and *y*-axis representing frequency

5.4 Clinical Quality Variables

The clinical quality variables like number of days of stay and number of visits to the hospital, for both the specialty and multispecialty cardiac care, are discussed as follows:

5.4.1 Number of Days of Stay

The number of days of stay is one of the important demographical factors ranging from 1 to 20 days.

For specialty cardiac care hospitals, from the data, in males it is 5–10 days of stay for 63% of respondents, followed by 1–5 days of stay for 21% of respondents.

In females it is 5–10 days of stay for 54% followed by 1–5 days as well as 10–15 days of stay constituting 22%.

For the multispecialty cardiac care hospitals, the number of days of stay in males is 10–15 days for 43% of respondents, followed by 5–10 days of stay for 31% of respondents. In females it is 10–15 days of stay for 44% followed by 5–10 days of stay constituting for 42% of respondents.

5.4.2   Number of Visits to the Hospital

The number of visits to the hospital ranges from 1 to 12 visits. For specialty cardiac care hospitals, in case of males, 3–6 visits were reported for constituting 53% of the respondents which is followed by 6–9 visits with 25% of males. But in females the data indicates 3–6 visits for 49% of respondents followed by 6–9 visits for 31% of respondents.

For multispecialty cardiac care hospitals, the number of visits to the hospital in case of males is 3–6 visits constituting the 47% of respondents which is followed by 1–3 visits for 34% of males. But in females it is 3–6 visits for 58% of respondents followed by 1–3 visits for 19% of respondents. It is depicted in Table 5.2.

5.5   Test of Significance for Clinical Quality Variables

The mean and standard deviation values are estimated for the clinical quality variables. The Z test has been administered to find out the significance of the clinical variables with respect to the gender and the type of specialty of the hospital at 0.01 significance level. Here, the null hypobook considered is:

H_0: There is no significant difference between the two means.

But in case of different sorts of hospitals, the H_0 is rejected and they are proven to be significant. In case of same traits of hospitals, the H_0 gets accepted, resulting in insignificance in their mean value. It is depicted in Table 5.3.

5.6   Results and Discussion

From Table 5.3, it is evident that the clinical variables when compared within the same sort of hospital are insignificant, whereas they are significant when compared with the other sort of hospital. The mean value for the number of days of stay for the gender male is 7.93 and 11.93, respectively, in specialty and multispecialty hospitals. Similarly the mean value for the number of days of stay for the gender female is 8.14 and 10.81, respectively, in specialty and multispecialty hospitals. It depicts that the male and female of specialty cardiac care hospitals are having less mean for 'number of days of stay'. It implies that the length of stay of patient in a hospital is less, i.e., the patient is cured quickly which results in his satisfaction. In addition, the mean of 'number of visits' to the hospital before the admission for both male (6.82) and female (7.02) is more in specialty cardiac care hospitals compared to that of a multispecialty cardiac care hospitals (4.77 and 5.35). It implies that more visits are portrayed for specialty cardiac care hospitals. It is also a positive indicator depicting the loyalty of the patients towards hospital.

Table 5.2 Table showing the data for clinical quality variables of specialty and multispecialty cardiac care hospitals

Clinical quality variables	Range	Specialty cardiac care		Multispecialty cardiac care	
		Frequency		Frequency	
		Male	Female	Male	Female
Number of days of stay	1–5	34	30	24	7
	5–10	103	74	69	58
	10–15	21	30	115	60
	15–20	4	2	60	12
Number of visits to the hospital	1–3	4	2	91	26
	3–6	88	66	126	80
	6–9	40	42	31	20
	9–12	32	26	20	11

Table 5.3 Table showing the comparison of clinical quality variables and their significance

Clinical quality variables				
1. Number of days of stay				
S. No	Comparison of clinical variables	Mean	Calculated 'Z' value	Significance test at 0.1 significance level
1	Male (specialty)	7.93	−2.645	Significant
	Male (multispecialty)	11.93		
2	Female (specialty)	8.14	−1.73	Significant
	Female (multispecialty)	10.81		
3	Male (specialty)	7.93	−0.15	Not significant
	Female (specialty)	8.14		
4	Male (multispecialty)	11.93	0.67	Not significant
	Female (multispecialty)	10.81		
2. Number of visits to the hospital				
5	Male (specialty)	6.82	3.23	Significant
	Male (multispecialty)	4.77		
6	Female (specialty)	7.02	2.409	Significant
	Female (multispecialty)	5.35		
7	Male (specialty)	6.82	−0.29	Not significant
	Female (specialty)	7.02		
8	Male (multispecialty)	4.77	−0.9006	Not significant
	Female (multispecialty)	5.35		

5.7   Conclusion

In this chapter the demographical indices like age and the gender have been analysed. In addition the clinical quality indicators like the length of the stay and the number of visits to the hospitals are analysed for both specialty and multispecialty cardiac care hospitals.

The results and discussions depict that in specialty cardiac hospitals, the length of stay is less, which will eventually lead to patient satisfaction. Likewise the number of visits to the hospital is more in case of specialty cardiac care hospitals indicating the patient loyalty. The specialty cardiac care hospitals are proven best with respect to demographical indices and clinical quality variables.

Chapter 6
Developing a Causal Model Using SEM

Contents

6.1   Introduction

SEM is a statistical technique for testing and estimating causal relations using a combination of statistical data and qualitative causal assumptions. This definition of SEM was articulated by the geneticist 'Sewall Wright', the economist 'Trygve Haavelmo' and the cognitive scientist 'Herbert Simon' and formally defined by 'Judea Pearl' using a calculus of counterfactuals.

Structural equation models (SEM) allow both confirmatory and exploratory modelling, meaning they are suited to both theory testing and theory development. Confirmatory modelling usually starts out with a hypobook that gets represented in a causal model. The concepts used in the model must then be operationalized to allow for the testing of relationships between the concepts in the model. The model

© Springer International Publishing AG 2018   41
S. Mohapatra et al., *Service Quality in Indian Hospitals*, Advances in Theory and
Practice of Emerging Markets, https://doi.org/10.1007/978-3-319-67888-7_6

is tested against the obtained measurement data to determine how well the model fits the data. The causal assumptions embedded in the model often have falsifiable implications which can be tested against the data. Among the strengths of SEM is its ability to construct latent variables: variables which are not measured directly but are estimated in the model from several measured variables each of which is predicted to 'tap into' the latent variables. This allows the modeller to explicitly capture the unreliability of measurement in the model, which in theory allows the structural relations between latent variables to be accurately estimated.

In SEM, the qualitative causal assumptions are represented by the missing variables in each equation, as well as vanishing covariance among some error terms. These assumptions are testable in experimental studies and must be confirmed judgmentally in observational studies.

6.2 Development of Causal Model

To fulfil the objective, a causal model was developed based on structural equation model (SEM) to determine the patient satisfaction of specialized heart care hospitals and multispecialty hospitals. Appendix 2 shows the macro view of the process, i.e. all the 41 indicators influencing the 10 dimensions and its influence on patient satisfaction. The structural model of SEM denotes the relationship between service quality dimensions and cardiac patient satisfaction. We can write a series of equations/statements that summarize its configuration. As such, we need to address the measurement model factor structure as shown in Appendix 3. As discussed in Chap. 4 and Sect 4.7.1, the summarization of measurement model structure is

$$Y = \lambda_y \eta + \varepsilon \tag{6.1}$$

The summarization of structural model as shown in Appendix 4 is

$$\eta = \Gamma \xi + \zeta \tag{6.2}$$

6.3 Data for SEM

For this study, the 154 hospitals listed by the central government health scheme rules of the Indian government are considered. Among 154 hospitals, 25% of the hospitals are targeted which constitutes 38 private hospitals offering cardiac services in India. The data is used for testing the hypobook and to meet the objective of deriving the order of preference of the dimensions influencing the satisfaction of cardiac patients. The study collected data from 10 speciality cardiac care hospitals and 18 multispecialty hospitals having cardiac care as one of their specialities. Respondents are patients suffering from cardiac diseases. 300 patients of speciality cardiac care hospitals and 405 patients of multispecialty hospitals provided data for the study. The sampling is a simple random sampling. This study used the validated questionnaire mentioned in Chap. 5 and collected responses on a 7-point Likert scale (ranging from 7, highly satisfied, to 1, highly dissatisfied). In random sampling, the randomness has been ensured by generating the random numbers, and the patient has been selected by the corresponding IP (inpatient) numbers of inpatients from different hospitals. The collected data is analysed to fulfil the objectives of the study.

6.4 Measurement Model

The measurement model is the part which relates measured variables to latent variables; here in our case, it relates the indicators to the service quality dimensions.

6.4.1 Formulation of Hypobook

Here, the hypobook is the influence of the indicators on their corresponding service quality dimensions. If the service quality dimension 'courtesy' is considered, then the hypobook associated with it will be:

- Politeness of physicians influences courtesy
- Politeness of nurses influences courtesy
- Politeness of hospital staff influences courtesy

Likewise the hypobook can be framed for all the indicators of ten service quality dimensions. The indicators included in ten dimensions are depicted in Appendix 5.

6.4.2 Data for Measurement Model

The first data set of speciality cardiac care hospitals is considered here. Data of 300 inpatients of 10 speciality cardiac care hospitals are taken. The data matrix of size [300 × 41] is given as input in to LISREL for the measurement model, and the model is run.

For the second set of data, the similar process is repeated. Here 405 inpatients of 18 multispecialty hospitals having cardiac care as one of its specialities provided the data. The data matrix of size [405 × 41] is fed as input in to LISREL for the measurement model, and the model is run.

6.4.3 Testing of Hypobook

The proposed model is analysed by using measurement model of SEM. The indicators comprise of the endogenous dependent variables (y) related to tangibility (y_1–y_8),accessibility (y_9–y_{13}),understanding (y_{14}–y_{16}),courtesy (y_{17}–y_{19}), reliability (y_{20}–y_{21}), security (y_{22}–y_{23}), credibility (y_{24}–y_{25}), responsiveness (y_{26}–y_{33}), communication (y_{34}–y_{36}) and competence (y_{37}–y_{41}). Appendixes 6 and 7 depict the point estimates and t-values of all y model variables representing speciality and multispecialty cardiac care hospitals ranging from 2.81 to 12.23 and also the range of 3.21 to 14.21 at the attained level of significance at 0.05, respectively. All the indicators are found out to be statistically significant from the analysis.

The obtained $\chi 2$ values are 2472.36 for speciality cardiac and 2931.67 for multispecialty cardiac hospitals with corresponding degrees of freedom 734 and 769. The high $\chi 2$ values reject the null hypobook, i.e. the model fits the data. But in measurement model analysis, the researchers consider other fit indices. In this study, the other fit indices like RMSEA (root mean square error of approximation), NFI (normed fit index), RMR (root mean square residual), GFI (goodness of fit index), AGFI (adjusted goodness of fit index) and PGFI (parsimony goodness of fit index) provided reasonably good result for the model and proves that the model fits the data. Thus the test of the model achieves a responsible fit. The values of fit indices are depicted in Table 6.1.

6.5 Structural Model

The study considers ten service quality dimensions identified by Parasuraman et al. (1985). They portrayed the essential dimensions on which the corporate hospitals can concentrate for satisfaction and retaining the patients effectively. The hypobook is formulated as:

- Tangibility influences patient satisfaction.

Likewise the ten hypobook were formulated for the structural model to measure the patient's satisfaction as shown in Table 6.2.

6.5.1 Data for Structural Model

The factor scores obtained from the measurement models are given as an input to the structural models for both speciality and multispecialty cardiac care hospitals.

Table 6.1 Table showing the fit indices of the measurement model

Fit index (speciality cardiac care)	Range	Obtained values	Fit
RMSEA	0.08–0.1	0.1	Mediocre fit
NFI	0.0–1.0	0.7	Good fit
RMR	0.0–1.0	0.1	Acceptable
GFI	0.0–1.0	0.68	Mediocre fit
AGFI	0.0–1.0	0.63	Mediocre fit
PGFI	>0.5	0.51	Acceptable
Fit index (multispecialty cardiac care)			
RMSEA	0.08–0.1	0.09	Mediocre fit
NFI	0.0–1.0	0.6	Good fit
RMR	0.0–1.0	0.1	Acceptable
GFI	0.0–1.0	0.7	Mediocre fit
AGFI	0.0–1.0	0.66	Mediocre fit
PGFI	>0.5	0.62	Acceptable

Table 6.2 Table projecting the hypobook

Hypobook
H1: Tangibility ------ patient satisfaction.
H2: Accessibility----- patient satisfaction
H3: Understanding ----patient satisfaction
H4: Courtesy ----patient satisfaction
H5: Reliability ----patient satisfaction
H6: Security ----patient satisfaction
H7: Credibility----patient satisfaction
H8: Responsiveness ---- patient satisfaction
H9: Communication ----patient satisfaction
H10: Competence ----patient satisfaction

6.5.2 Testing of Hypobook

The point estimates and t-values of all the service quality dimensions representing speciality cardiac care hospitals ranging from −9.92 to 24.18 with attained level of significance at 0.05 and the range of −27.01 to 23.61 at 0.05 significance level for multispecialty cardiac hospitals are depicted in Table 6.3.

The results of the structural model exhibit that all the path coefficient values are statistically significant at $p < 0.05$. So, the structural model supports all ten hypobook. The influence of patient satisfaction on all the ten dimensions *Tangibility, Accessibility, Understanding, Courtesy, Reliability, Security, Credibility, Responsiveness, Communication and Competence* has been proved by hypobook H1, H2, H3, H4, H5, H6, H7, H8, H9 and H10 for both speciality cardiac care ($H1_s$, $H2_s$, $H3_s$, $H4_s$, $H5_s$, $H6_s$, $H7_s$, $H8_s$, $H9_s$, $H10_s$) and multispecialty hospitals ($H1_m$,

Table 6.3 Table representing the significance of the hypobook

Causal path (specialty cardiac care hospitals)	Hypobook	Point estimate	t-value	Hypobook Support
Tangibility----patient satisfaction	H1$_s$	1.10	23.22	Significant
Accessibility---- patient satisfaction	H2$_s$	1.14	24.18	Significant
Understanding --- patient satisfaction	H3$_s$	1.05	21.90	Significant
Courtesy---- patient satisfaction	H4$_s$	0.60	11.08	Significant
Reliability ----- patient satisfaction	H5$_s$	0.05	0.86	Significant
Security---- patient satisfaction	H6$_s$	−0.079	−9.92	Significant
Credibility ---- patient satisfaction	H7$_s$	0.28	4.93	Significant
Responsiveness---- patient satisfaction	H8$_s$	0.61	11.26	Significant
Communication---patient satisfaction	H9$_s$	1.05	9.94	Significant
Competence --- patient satisfaction	H10$_s$	0.46	8.26	Significant
Causal path (multispecialty cardiac care hospitals)				
Tangibility----patient satisfaction	H1$_m$	0.26	5.25	Significant
Accessibility ---- patient satisfaction	H2$_m$	0.45	9.37	Significant
Understanding --- patient satisfaction	H3$_m$	1.05	23.61	Significant
Courtesy ---- patient satisfaction	H4$_m$	−0.72	−16.56	Significant
Reliability ----- patient satisfaction	H5$_m$	−0.43	−8.89	Significant
Security ---- patient satisfaction	H6$_m$	−0.98	−27.01	Significant
Credibility ---- patient satisfaction	H7$_m$	−0.47	−10.03	Significant
Responsiveness ---- patient satisfaction	H8$_m$	−1.03	−26.41	Significant
Communication---patient satisfaction	H9$_m$	−0.85	−21.19	Significant
Competence --- patient satisfaction	H10$_m$	−1.02	−26.67	Significant

H2$_m$, H3$_m$, H4$_m$, H5$_m$, H6$_m$, H7$_m$, H8$_m$, H9$_m$, H10$_m$). Thus, the SEM model ensures that the proposed model is consistent and gains acceptable level. The study tested all the hypobook and proved them. The χ^2 value obtained for multispecialty hospitals is 5371.62 with 531.62 degrees of freedom. Similarly, for cardiac speciality hospitals, the χ^2 value obtained is 2461.23 with 246.23 degrees of freedom. Both these values are substantially high, and so the null hypobook, stating that the model fits the data, is rejected. However, on the analysis of the fit indices including RMSEA, NFI, RMR, GFI, AGFI and PFI, we get favourable results with values ranging from acceptable levels to very good fits. In Table 6.4, the obtained fit values, the standard ranges for the fit values and their corresponding categorization are tabulated for both speciality cardiac care and multispecialty hospitals.

From the above table, based on the standard range values and the fitness level achieved for each of the fit indices, it can be concluded that the results of the SEM model are acceptable. Appendix 8 (a, b, c, d) shows the path diagrams, i.e. the LISREL outputs representing the measurement model and structural model for both speciality cardiac care and the multispecialty hospitals.

Table 6.4 Table showing the fit indices of the structural model

Fit index (speciality cardiac care)	Range	Obtained value	Fit
RMSEA	0.08–0.1	0.1	Mediocre fit
NFI	0.0–1.0	0.99	Best fit
RMR	0.0–1.0	0.039	Acceptable fit
GFI	0.0–1.0	0.99	Good fit
AGFI	0.0–1.0	0.98	Acceptable fit
PGFI	>0.5	0.63	Acceptable fit
Fit index (multispecialty cardiac care)			
RMSEA	<0.05	0.03	Best fit
NFI	0.0–1.0	0.99	Best fit
RMR	0.0–1.0	0.98	Mediocre fit
GFI	0.0–1.0	0.98	Good fit
AGFI	0.0–1.0	0.96	Acceptable fit
PGFI	>0.5	0.62	Acceptable fit

6.6 Prioritization of Dimensions

The study analysed the magnitude of the path coefficient value from the output of causal model of speciality cardiac care hospitals and arrived at the ranking of each dimension based on the corresponding path estimate values. This is done because path estimate is the measure of the relationship between the service quality dimension and the patient satisfaction. Tables 6.5 and 6.6 depict the ranking of dimensions of multispecialty and speciality cardiac care hospitals, respectively.

6.7 Cluster Analysis

We conducted Spearman's rank correlation test on the ranked data, and we arrived at a rank correlation coefficient of 0.468 with two-tailed test at 0.01 level of significance. This proves that there is a difference in ranking between the speciality cardiac care hospitals and multispecialty hospitals.

So, instead of treating each dimension separately for comparison, it is better to form a cluster, where each of its elements gets the equal priority. This study then clusters all the ranked dimensions of speciality cardiac care hospitals using K-means clustering. The reason for clustering of dimensions is that the path coefficients of the dimensions have very minimal differences between them. By considering the prominent differences in the path coefficient values, the study formed three clusters for speciality cardiac care hospitals. The obtained path coefficient values are given as input into K-means clustering algorithm. Table 6.7 depicts the members of the clusters for speciality cardiac care hospitals. The same is done for multispecialty hospitals too, and four clusters are formed including all the ten dimensions.

Table 6.5 Path estimates and ranking of multispecialty hospital

Factors	Path estimate	Ranking
Tangibility	0.26	3
Accessibility	0.45	2
Understanding	1.05	1
Courtesy	−0.72	6
Reliability	−0.43	4
Security	−0.98	8
Credibility	−0.47	5
Responsiveness	−1.03	10
Communication	−0.85	7
Competence	−1.02	9

Table 6.6 Path estimates and ranking of specialty cardiac care hospitals

Factors	Path estimate scores	Ranking
Tangibility	1.10	2
Accessibility	1.14	1
Understanding	1.05	3
Courtesy	0.60	6
Reliability	0.05	9
Security	−0.079	10
Credibility	0.28	8
Responsiveness	0.61	5
Communication	1.05	3
Competence	0.46	7

Table 6.7 Clustering of ten dimensions for speciality cardiac care hospitals

Cluster	Factors
I	Accessibility Tangibility Understanding Communication
II	Responsiveness Courtesy Competence Credibility
III	Reliability Security

A panel of experts comprising leading cardiologists, directors of speciality cardiac care hospitals, discussed these clustered factors of both speciality cardiac hospitals and multispecialty hospitals. They scrutinized the prioritization of dimensions, by considering their ranking and its clustering. They concluded that the order of preference of dimensions for speciality cardiac care hospitals can be set as a benchmark for multispecialty hospitals to compare. The three clusters obtained are:

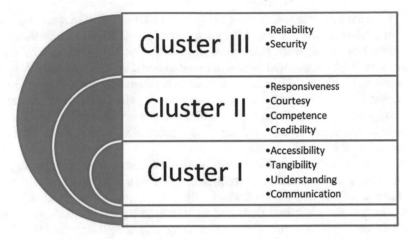

Fig. 6.1 Pictographical representation of clustering of service quality dimensions of specialty cardiac care hospitals

(a) *Cluster I* – consisting of four service quality dimensions, accessibility, tangibility, understanding and communication.
(b) *Cluster II* – consisting of four service quality dimensions responsiveness, courtesy, competence and credibility.
(c) *Cluster III* – consisting of two service quality dimensions, reliability and security as shown in Fig. 6.1.

In the process of analysing the importance of the indicators related to each dimensions, we can enumerate the following:

The four dimensions (accessibility, tangibility, understanding, communication) fall in the first cluster and get the highest priority when compared with the remaining service quality dimensions.

Even a determinant like availability of visitor parking plays a role in patient's satisfaction. In addition factors like availability of information regarding patient's condition, ease of getting hold of hospital personnel on phone, availability of meals and sleeping accommodation to the patient's visitors play a significant role in determining the patient's satisfaction. As cardiac care is critical care, *accessibility* is the most highly preferred service quality dimension.

The facilities, infrastructure and appearances matter a lot. A clean and hygienic environment will protect the patient from communicable diseases or nosocomial infections and also satisfies him. A pleasant environment, calm and soothing zone will also improve the recovery of patient. So tangibility matters in curing a patient.

A thorough concern to the patient and their family as well as visitors determines the patient satisfaction. Even the amount of time spent by the staff to get to know about the patient's condition also matters with respect to satisfaction of the patient. Understanding a patient's need along with his attendant's needs look like a minor issue, but it will turn out into a major issue in determining the overall satisfaction of the patients. The hospitals need to understand and attend to such issues.

Explanation about the condition of the patient and the type of treatment given to him by the hospital staff along with the adequacy of instructions given at the time of release on how to take care determines the satisfaction of a patient. The doctor should furnish all the required details in order to boost up the confidence levels in patients to fight against the disease. A well communicative doctor is the best doctor. Especially in cardiac patients, apart from the physical pain, mental stress and agony also play a major role. Effective communication can act as a palliative cure. So, effective communication and soothing of the patients will relax them from such psychological phobias and trauma.

As treatment is the need of the hour, immediate *responsiveness* of the hospital staff towards a cardiac patient is prerequisite, along with it the *courtesy* of the staff towards the patients and their attendants, the *competence* of the doctors and the *credibility*, i.e. the advertised treatment as promised by the hospital, will highly satisfy the cardiac patient. So, all these service quality dimensions form the second cluster, and the following discussion explains the same:

The cardiac diseases are very critical, even few seconds matter during emergencies, so the doctors term these as golden minutes and platinum seconds, because it will decide the life of the patient. The responsiveness of the nurses and physicians towards the need of the patient is a crucial satisfaction factor. Also mainly the waiting time for the medical investigations and tests, refund, speed and ease of admissions and discharge processes will influence patient satisfaction staunchly. Here in case of cardiac patients, the immediate response is of utmost importance.

Courtesy is also an essential factor. The politeness of the physicians, nurses and other staff reflect their attention to the patients, and they will perceive that they get more preference and importance than the others; such positive feeling helps in satisfying the patients.

Competence in a patient's view is when a patient realizes the competence of the doctor if the doctor relieves him from his infliction. For example, a patient will rank a nurse's act of injecting the drug in a soothing and painless manner as the most competent and skilful act. So competence in the view of cardiac patients will be nothing other than his relief from pain and his immediate soothing after the occurrence of a disease. In addition, the skill of the nurses, lab investigators and the nonclinical staff of insurance departments and billing determines the patient satisfaction.

Credibility is also a major factor in satisfying a patient. The hospitals must advertise and promote them in a reasonable way and should keep up all they have promised to deliver; sometimes the patients will be delighted if they get much more than their expectations. So meeting the expectations of patients is also a key factor; failure may lead to dissatisfaction. The ability of the hospital to deliver what was promised in its advertising and whether the treatment the patient have undergone is on par with his expectations will influence the patient satisfaction.

Depending on the treatment received, the patients will frame their opinion of whether the hospital is *reliable* and if they derive a sense of *security* from the association. The patients will consider these factors after the completion of the treatment. So these two service quality dimensions form the third cluster. The explanation is enumerated as follows:

Reliability is the factor which will keep up the patient–hospital relationship. If the patient feels that he has received the required treatment and the performance of hospital is up to his expectations, he will be the loyal customer to it. In case of cardiac patients, the loyalty and the hospital patient relationship will be very high. Even the performance of services when they were supposed to be performed and also in the way they would be performed should satisfy a patient.

The other dimension, namely, *security*, is also necessary because, here, the complexity of the disease and fear of life threat towards a cardiac disease will be comparatively high. Many cardiologists opine that most commonly the cardiac patients or their attendants ask for the risk associated with the disease and their security of well-being after the treatment in the hospital. The sense of well-being and the sense of security from physical harm felt in the hospital by the patient are also important factors in patient satisfaction.

6.8   Results and Discussion

As discussed in Sect. 6.7, the panel of experts concluded the specialty cardiac care as a bench mark for service quality and to satisfy a patient. So, a comparative study has been carried out between specialty cardiac care hospitals and multispecialty cardiac hospitals. The study analysed the differences of ranking between the two, and the service quality dimensions carrying a value of '−2' and less than '−2' are identified for recommended measures. (Table 6.8 shows the same.)

The following equation enables to arrive at the rank difference:

Rank difference = Specialty cardiac care ranking – Multispecialty ranking

Table 6.8 Table showing the rankings and rank differences

Service quality dimensions	Ranking of factors in speciality cardiac care hospitals	Ranking of factors in multispecialty hospitals having cardiac care as one of their speciality	Rank difference
Tangibility	2	3	−1
Accessibility	1	2	−1
Understanding	3	1	+2
Courtesy	6	6	0
Reliability	9	4	+5
Security	10	8	+2
Credibility	8	5	+3
Responsiveness	5	10	−5
Communication	3	7	−4
Competence	7	9	−2

In the case of multispecialty hospitals, the important dimensions like responsiveness (−5), competence (−2) and communication (−4) bear the negative value with significant differences.

The dimension *communication* gets a high priority in cluster I for specialized cardiac care hospitals. But in the case of multispecialty hospitals, it gets least preference status. *Communication* is considered as an important dimension in cardiac care. The doctors have to properly communicate the seriousness of the disease, the precautions needed, the post-hospitalization care, etc. to satisfy a patient. Specialized cardiac care hospitals have more concern about *communication* than that of the multispecialty hospitals.

The study found the dimensions *responsiveness* and *competence* are important in cluster II for specialized cardiac care hospitals. But in multispecialty hospitals, both these dimensions got the least preference. Patients consider *responsiveness* as one of the important dimensions. They require immediate and timely response for cardiac problems to decrease their critical levels. Specialized cardiac hospitals are considerably showing more *responsiveness* than that of multispecialty hospitals. Likewise *competence* of doctors and other clinical staff is the best considerable dimension in order to satisfy a patient. Specialized cardiac hospitals are keen at this and comparatively have all the required competent staff. Hence patients prefer specialized cardiac care hospitals most.

The implications of this study are the multispecialty cardiac hospitals that can categorize their service delivery by keeping in view the top prioritized dimensions as per the analysis. They can overcome the gaps in service delivery by following the recommendations addressed to them in order to satisfy their patients in every possible aspect.

6.9   Conclusion

In this chapter, a causal model has been developed using structural equation modelling. Individual models has been developed for both specialty and multispecialty cardiac care hospitals. Causal model tested the fit of the model; the path estimate values and latent scores are obtained from causal model which are analysed further. By considering the path estimate scores obtained from the model, the service quality dimensions are clustered. Further they are prioritized and ranked. Specialty cardiac care is regarded as the benchmark for superior service quality and excellent patient satisfaction. So, by considering the specialty cardiac care hospitals as a benchmark, the individual ranks of service quality dimensions of multispecialty cardiac care hospitals have been compared with it. The results obtained were discussed in detail.

Chapter 7
Developing a Classification Model Using ANN

Contents

7.1 Introduction

An artificial neural network is a mathematical model inspired by biological neural networks. A neural network consists of an interconnected group of artificial neurons, and it processes information using a connectionist approach to computation. In most cases, a neural network is an adaptive system changing its structure during a learning phase. Neural networks are used for determining complex relationships between inputs and outputs or to find patterns in data. The inspiration for neural networks came from examination of the central nervous system. In an artificial neural network, simple artificial nodes, called 'neurons', 'processing elements' or 'units', are connected together to form a network which mimics a biological neural network.

There is no single formal definition of what an artificial neural network is. Generally, it involves a network of simple processing elements exhibiting complex global behaviour determined by examining the connections between the processing elements and element parameters. Artificial neural networks are used with algorithms designed to alter the strength of the connections in the network to produce a desired signal flow.

© Springer International Publishing AG 2018
S. Mohapatra et al., *Service Quality in Indian Hospitals*, Advances in Theory and
Practice of Emerging Markets, https://doi.org/10.1007/978-3-319-67888-7_7

7.2 Neural Network

To develop a classification model, the study adopts multilayer feed-forward network with back propagation neural network architecture. The study uses back propagation to train the data. The two neural network models (i) for speciality cardiac care hospitals and (ii) for multispecialty hospitals are developed for determining cardiac patient satisfaction. Input, hidden and output layers are the three layers of a neural network. Neurons are the computational units of the layer. The input neurons are the number of input variables. There is a link between the input layer neurons and the hidden layer neurons, and the weights on these links are called input–hidden layer weights. There is a link between the hidden layer neuron and the output layer neurons, and the weights on these links are the output layer weights. The study used these weights to compute the respective layer output. The same procedure is carried out for both the speciality cardiac and multispecialty hospitals.

7.3 Training and Testing of Model Using Neural Network

The study used MATLAB to train the neural network models. Input and output data used to train the patient satisfaction model are considered as follows:

Input Data The latent variable score obtained from causal model using LISREL 8.8 for individual factors of service quality dimensions becomes the input data.

Output Data LISREL 8.8 is used to calculate the factor scores. This computed latent patient satisfaction factor score becomes the output data for the corresponding input values.

For example, for m observations and n service quality dimensions (in our case, for specialized cardiac care hospitals, m is 300, and for multispecialty hospitals, m is 405 and n is 10) for cardiac patient satisfaction, the input and output matrices are as follows:

$$
\begin{pmatrix}
X_{11}\ X_{12}\ X_{13}\ X_{14}\ldots\ldots\ldots X_{1n} \\
X_{21}\ X_{22}\ X_{23}\ X_{24}\ldots\ldots\ldots X_{2n} \\
X_{m1}\ X_{m1}\ X_{m3}\ X_{m4}\ldots\ldots\ldots X_{mn}
\end{pmatrix}
\begin{pmatrix}
F_1 \\
F_2 \\
F_m
\end{pmatrix}
$$

Input data matrix $(m \times n)$ Output data matrix $(m \times 1)$

(Latent factor score of dimensions)   (Latent factor score of patient satisfaction)

where X_{11}, X_{12}, $X_{13}\ldots X_{1n}$ are the latent variable scores for the n dimensions and F_1 is the latent factor score of the patient satisfaction. Likewise F_2, $F_3\ldots F_m$ are the corresponding latent factor scores of the observed data. The empirical formula (Ying Wang et al.) is the basis to calculate the number of hidden neurons.

$$m = n + 0.618 \times (n-1)$$

where m is the number of hidden neurons and n is the number of input layer neurons. Here n is 10. Using the formula, the study obtained 16 hidden neurons.

The study provided the input and output data and used MATLAB to train the neural network models. The algorithm used for training the network model using MATLAB is as follows:

1. Define the number of training and testing data sets.
2. Input the training data. Each training data consists of a pair of observed data, and the study used SEM to calculate the latent variable scores.
3. Normalize the input and output data between 0 and 1 for better working of the neural network model.
4. Define the number of hidden neurons based on the input neurons.
5. Define the neural network training function for the input, hidden and output neurons.
6. Define the parameter values like learning rate, moment coefficient and number of epochs.
7. The back propagation model computing input and output values of the various layer nodes is as follows:

   - Compute the output of the input layer. The output is same as the input for a linear activation function.
   - Compute the input of the hidden layer neurons by multiplying the weights of synapses connecting input neurons and hidden neurons with the output of the input layer.
   - Evaluate the output of the hidden layer neurons using activation function.
   - Compute the input of the output layer neurons by multiplying the weights of synapses connecting hidden neurons and output neurons with the output of the hidden layer neurons.
   - Evaluate the output of the output layer neurons using activation function.

8. Calculate the error value by comparing the actual output values with the calculated output values.
9. Repeat the training process till the error attains minimum acceptable limit by varying the learning rate, moment coefficient and number of epochs.

The models get stabilized at some learning rate and moment coefficient. Tables 7.1 and 7.2 of specialty and multispecialty hospitals depict the parameter values of model in its stable state. The corresponding weights of input to hidden layer and hidden to output layer are shown in Appendices 9, 10, 11, and 12. The entire neural network framework is depicted in Appendix 13.

The study considers the latent factor score as the cardiac patient satisfaction score based on the service quality dimensions. In this model, the threshold value for determining patient satisfaction is '0' and ranges from −1 to +1. If a patient scores more than threshold value, i.e. 0, he is a satisfied patient, and if he scores less than

Table 7.1 Model parameter
values of specialty cardiac
care hospitals

No. of epochs	38,000
Learning rate	0.65
Moment coefficient	0. 5
MSE	0.002

Table 7.2 Model parameter
values of multispecialty
cardiac care hospitals

No. of epochs	38,000
Learning rate	0.7
Moment coefficient	0. 65
MSE	0.002

0, then he is a dissatisfied patient. The magnitude of the satisfaction score tells us whether the patient is highly satisfied or not.

7.4 Significance of Weights

Before discussing about the satisfaction level of patients, it is appropriate to justify the importance of weights in the neural network. Figure 7.1 shows the neural network framework.

Let us consider that X_{35} and X_{45} are the output of the hidden neurons. The weights are assumed to be W_{35} and W_{45} and given the values are 0.2 and −0.5, respectively. The activation function used in this model is sigmoidal activation function with zero bias. The table shows the values of three instances:

- Weights taken as such
- Decreasing weights
- Increasing weights

From the values obtained, it is proved that if the value of weights increases, the output value is increasing and vice versa. So, it signifies that weights obtained

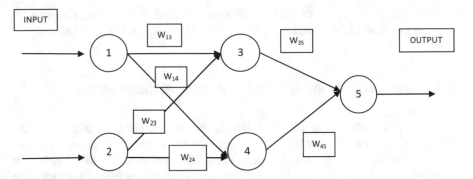

Fig. 7.1 Neural network framework

Table 7.3 Influence of weights on output

X_{35}	X_{45}	Instance	W_{35}	W_{45}	$1/1 + e^{-z}$
0.5448	0.505	1. Same	0.2	−0.5	0.4642
		2. Decreasing	0.1	−0.6	0.4382
		3. Increasing	0.3	−0.4	0.4903

between the hidden neurons and the output neuron in neural network depict the strength of the output neuron, and it is shown in Table 7.3.

The output from the classification model, i.e. the neural network weights, is used for a comparative analysis. As had been evidenced earlier, the weights have an influence on the output, in this case, the patient satisfaction.

The range of the contribution level for satisfaction is arrived from the weights representing the bondage between hidden and the output neurons. This is done through the calculation of the aggregate lowest, highest, mean and spread values, and the difference between the aggregate highest and lowest values is the spread. The steps involved in arriving at the spread are shown as follows:

Among the weights of each service quality dimension to the corresponding hidden and output neurons, the highest weight, the lowest weight and the mean weight values are considered for all ten dimensions.

Calculate the sum of all the lowest weights, highest weights mean weight values and the spread for each dimension to arrive at corresponding aggregate values.

A comparative table is drawn by highlighting all the values for both speciality and multispecialty cardiac hospitals.

The procedure is followed for both the specialty cardiac care hospitals and multispecialty hospitals. The obtained values are tabulated in Table 7.4 as follows:

7.5   Comparative Study on Significance of Satisfaction

Table 7.5 is constructed by selecting the highest weight, mean weight and lowest weight as measures to show the contribution of each dimension to patient satisfaction. They are obtained by considering all the ten dimensions as a whole. The lowest contribution is the aggregate of the lowest weights of all the ten dimensions. The highest contribution is the aggregate of the highest weights of all the ten dimensions. Mean contribution is the aggregate of the mean of both the lowest and the highest contributions.

The graphical representation of them is shown in Figs 7.2 and 7.3.

7.6   Validation of the Model

The established predictive model has to be checked for its validity. For this, the study took a sample data of 30% for both specialty cardiac care and multispecialty hospitals as a sample. After running the model, the predicted values were compared against actual values. A confusion matrix is framed to test the apparent error rate and accuracy of the stabilized predictive model. The confusion matrices are depicted in Tables 7.6 and 7.7 as follows:

The study calculated apparent error rate of 4.4% and an accuracy of 95.6% for the speciality cardiac care hospitals.

The study calculated apparent error rate of 11.4% and an accuracy of 88.6% for the multispecialty hospitals.

7.7   Results

It is concluded that the contribution for satisfaction is more from specialized cardiac care hospitals as expected, with a maximal aggregate score of 8.96 compared to that of multispecialty hospitals having a maximal aggregate score of 7.93. The mean score is also high for speciality hospital, but the spread of the aggregate values shows that the speciality hospitals have comparatively more spread than the multispecialty hospitals. This is an indication that the contribution dimension of dissatisfaction of patients in the case of speciality cardiac hospitals is comparatively more than the dissatisfaction of multispecialty hospitals. This may be due to over expectation of the patients. This can be due to the varied patient categorization specified to cardiac diseases and also due to the large inflow of patients to the speciality cardiac

Table 7.4 The lowest and highest path weights from input neurons to the hidden neurons of both the speciality cardiac care and multispecialty hospitals

Dimension	No. of weights from hidden to output neurons	Specialty cardiac care hospitals				Multispecialty cardiac hospitals			
		Lowest contribution	Mean contribution	Highest contribution	Spread	Lowest contribution	Mean contribution	Highest contribution	Spread
L1 (tangibility)	16	−0.78	0.14	0.68	1.46	−0.73	0.144	0.91	1.64
L2 (accessibility)	16	−0.74	0.24	1.64	2.38	−0.99	0.12	0.84	1.83
L3 (understanding)	16	−0.92	−0.25	0.34	1.26	−1.13	−0.078	0.67	1.80
L4 (courtesy)	16	−1.44	−0.13	1.07	2.51	−0.68	0.067	0.79	1.47
L5 (reliability)	16	−0.94	0.04	1.14	2.08	−0.67	−0.083	0.88	1.55
L6 (security)	16	−0.76	0.06	0.89	1.65	−0.83	0.053	0.77	1.60
L7 (credibility)	16	−0.65	0.203	0.91	1.56	−0.97	−0.084	0.76	1.73
L8(responsiveness)	16	−1.27	−0.203	0.82	2.09	−1.15	0.006	0.77	1.92
L9 (communication)	16	−0.92	0.016	0.75	1.67	−0.86	−0.045	0.85	1.71
L10 (competence)	16	−0.89	−0.24	0.72	1.61	−0.95	−0.28	0.69	1.64
Aggregate		**−9.31**	**−0.124**	**8.96**	**18.27**	**−8.96**	**−0.18**	**7.93**	**16.89**

Table 7.5 Table showing the lowest, mean and highest satisfaction range of both the speciality cardiac care and multispecialty hospitals by considering all the ten dimensions

Speciality cardiac care hospitals		Spread	Multispecialty cardiac hospitals		Spread
Lowest contribution	−9.31	18.27	Lowest contribution	−8.96	16.89
Mean contribution	−0.124		Mean contribution	−0.18	
Highest contribution	8.96		Highest contribution	7.93	

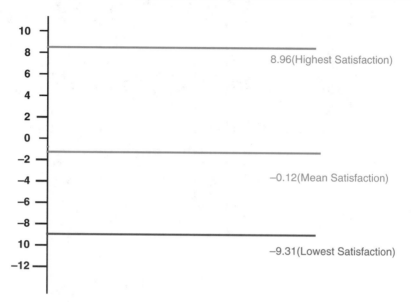

Fig. 7.2 Graph showing the lowest, mean and highest satisfaction range of the speciality cardiac care hospitals

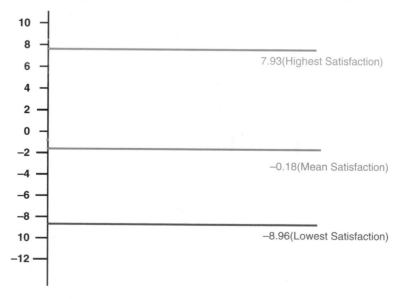

Fig. 7.3 Graph showing the lowest, mean and highest satisfaction range of the multispeciality cardiac care hospitals

Table 7.6 Confusion matrix using ANN for cardiac specialty hospitals

Confusion matrix for cardiac care hospitals (30% of 300 sample = 90)		**Predicted**		
		Satisfied	*Dissatisfied*	
Actual	*Satisfied*	48	4	*52*
	Dissatisfied	0	38	*38*

Table 7.7 Confusion matrix using ANN for multispecialty hospitals

Confusion matrix for multispecialty hospitals (30% of 405 sample = 122)		**Predicted**		
		Satisfied	*Dissatisfied*	
Actual	*Satisfied*	87	14	*101*
	Dissatisfied	0	21	*21*

care hospitals. As the patients come with high levels of expectation to the speciality cardiac care hospitals, even a minor deviation in the delivery of services may amplify their dissatisfaction.

The ANN models of both the specialty cardiac care and multispecialty hospitals have been validated using confusion matrices, and the apparent error rates are found to be 4.4% and 11.4%, respectively.

7.8   Conclusion

In this chapter, a classification model has been developed using artificial neural networking. The latent scores obtained from the SEM are considered as the data to the classification model. It is trained and tested with the data. The weights obtained are analysed further. The importance of the weights has been determined and the aggregate weights were calculated. In addition, the spread for both specialty and multispecialty hospitals has been verified which revealed that the patients of specialty cardiac care were highly satisfied compared to that of multispecialty cardiac care hospitals. The models were validated using confusion matrices.

Chapter 8
Developing a Classification Model Using SVM

Contents

8.1 Introduction

Support vector machines have established themselves as a standard data mining and machine learning tool. It is based on advances in statistical learning theory and finds a wide range of application in real-world situations like text categorization, handwritten character recognition, image classification, bio-sequences analysis, etc.

The four basic concepts that are involved in the understanding of an SVM are (i) separating hyperplane, (ii) maximum-margin hyperplane, (iii) soft margin and (iv) kernel function. The design of the technique is to draw a plane in such a way that the data is classified on either side of the separating hyperplane. The SVM, however, is different from other hyperplane-based classifiers by virtue of how the hyperplane is selected. The separating hyperplane is unique in nature as it will separate the two classes by adopting the maximal distance from any of the given data point. If we define the distance from the separating hyperplane to the nearest data vector as the margin of the hyperplane, then the SVM selects the maximum-margin separating hyperplane. The selection of such a hyperplane greatly enhances the ability of SVM to predict the right classification of a new data point. Any new data can then be mapped into either side of the separating hyperplane and so help predict the category to which the data belong.

© Springer International Publishing AG 2018   63
S. Mohapatra et al., *Service Quality in Indian Hospitals*, Advances in Theory and
Practice of Emerging Markets, https://doi.org/10.1007/978-3-319-67888-7_8

SVM can be defined as a method for the creation of an optimal hyperplane in a multidimensional space such that the hyperplane separates the two categories and has the lowest possible misclassification error (Burges 1998). The hyperplane has the lowest misclassification error when it has the largest possible margin between the hyperplane and the nearest plot in the training set on either side of the hyperplane. Such a hyperplane can be called the maximum-margin hyperplane.

8.2 Support Vector Machine

The support vector machine (SVM) is the one of the data mining techniques we are adopting to classify the cardiac patient satisfaction. The broad categorization of SVMs is as follows:

(a) Linearly separable classifier
(b) Linear inseparable classifier
(c) Nonlinear classifier

In this paper, SVMs are used to classify a cardiac patient as 'satisfied' or 'dissatisfied' using SPSS PASW modeller 14.2.

For analysis of data, using nonlinear classifier method is apt because the randomness of the data creates more misclassification while we use linear classifier to classify the data into two groups.

The dual form of the decision function for an SVM (Vapnik 1998) can be stated as:

$$\min_\alpha L_D = \frac{1}{2}\sum_{i,j=1}^{n} a_i \alpha_j y_i y_j K\left(x_i, x_j\right) - \sum_{i=1}^{n} \alpha_i$$

Subject to the constraint that:

$$0 \le \alpha_i \le C, \quad i = 1,\ldots,n \quad \text{and} \quad \sum_{i=1}^{n} \alpha_i y_i = 0$$

Maximum-margin hyperplane can be defined by solving this equation which will separate the data into two categories. Once an optimal hyperplane that separates one class from the other is constructed, classification decision function is given by the following equation:

$$f(y) = sign\left(\sum_{i=1}^{sv} \alpha_i y_i k\left(x, x_{sv}\right) + b \right) \qquad (8.1)$$

Here, in Eq. (8.1), $k(x, x_{sv})$ represents the kernel function of a nonlinear classifier, and 'sv' denotes the number of support vectors. As we use RBF kernel function, (8.1) can be written as:

$$f(y) = sign\left(\sum_{i=1}^{sv} \alpha_i y_i e^{-\gamma \|x_i - x_j\|^2} + b\right)$$

The calculated α value and the corresponding γ value are substituted along with the values of x and b to obtain the result. Here the sign of the result is an important component in classifying the patient but not the result. Depending on the sign obtained, cardiac patients can be classified in to either as 'satisfied' or 'dissatisfied'.

The SVM procedure is carried out as stated below:

1. Define the input x_i, where $i = 1...n$ and output $y_i \in \{-1, +1\}_{i=1....n}$.
2. Define the training and testing sets of data.
3. Use nonlinear SVM classifier.
4. Consider RBF kernel, $k(x_i, x_j) = e^{-\gamma \|xi - xj\|2}$.
5. Compute the parameter C and γ.
6. Run SVM in SPSS modeller for each computed value of c and γ till stabilization is attained.
7. Observe the output and categorize all data points having $y_i = -1$ as a dissatisfied patient and $y_i = +1$ as a satisfied patient.

8.3 Data

The input to the SVM is the latent score set obtained from the lower order model using SEM and the output is the actual values of patient satisfaction. The input matrix for the specialty cardiac hospitals is the latent score matrix of $[300 \times 10]$ and the output matrix is $[300 \times 1]$. For multispecialty cardiac care hospitals, the input data is $[405 \times 10]$ and output matrix is $[405 \times 1]$. Here 70% of the data, i.e. 210 for specialty cardiac hospitals and 283 for multispecialty hospitals, is given as training data, and 30% of the data, i.e. 90 for specialty cardiac hospitals and 122 for multispecialty cardiac care hospitals, is given as testing data for the model to run. Thus organized data is given as an input in the SPSS modeller software. The model gets stabilized at particular c (parameter estimation) and γ values. Here, in this case, the c values for both the specialty and multispecialty cardiac hospitals are 9, and the γ value is 0.6 and 0.5, respectively.

8.4 Validation of the Classification Models

In order to validate the SVM model, a confusion matrix is constructed. The confusion matrix for the study took a sample data of 30% for both specialty cardiac care and multispecialty hospitals. Here a comparison of the actual values with that of

predicted values is portrayed in a tabular form. A confusion matrix is framed to find
the apparent error rate and accuracy of the stabilized model. The study has calculated apparent error rate of testing data for both the specialty and multispecialty
hospitals. They are depicted in Tables 8.1 and 8.2.

The apparent error rate for specialty cardiac care hospitals is 3.3% with an accuracy rate of 96.7%.

The apparent error rate for multispecialty cardiac care hospitals is 9.01% with an
accuracy rate of 90.99%.

8.5   Comparison of ANN and SVM Using Confusion Matrices

In this study, both ANN and SVM are considered for classification of cardiac
patients of both specialty and multispecialty hospitals into either 'satisfied' or 'dissatisfied'. The study validated the classification techniques using confusion matrix.
The apparent error rate comparison of ANN and SVM techniques are shown in
Table 8.3.

It is obvious that the apparent error rate is comparatively less for the SVM when
compared with that of ANN. So, for this study, as the apparent error rate is comparatively less for SVM and the accuracy is more, it is considered as the best classification technique among the two.

Table 8.1 Confusion matrix using SVM for cardiac specialty hospitals

Confusion matrix for cardiac care hospitals (30% of 300 sample = 90)		**Predicted**		
		Satisfied	*Dissatisfied*	
Actual	*Satisfied*	51	3	**54**
	Dissatisfied	0	36	**36**

Table 8.2 Confusion matrix using SVM for cardiac multispecialty hospitals

Confusion matrix for multispecialty hospitals (30% of 405 sample = 122)		**Predicted**		
		Satisfied	*Dissatisfied*	
Actual	*Satisfied*	91	11	**102**
	Dissatisfied	0	20	**20**

Table 8.3 Apparent error rate comparison of ANN and SVM techniques

	ANN	SVM
Specialty	4.4%	3.3%
Multispecialty	11.4%	9.01%

Chapter 9
Summary and Conclusion

Contents

9.1   Discussions

In this chapter, we analyse and discuss the results from statistical analysis.

SVM is used in developing a classification model. It gets stabilized at some c and γ value. In order to validate the model confusion, matrices were depicted. SVM has shown low apparent error rate compared to that of ANN. So, this study proves that the SVM is the best data mining technique in classification when compared with ANN. It is comparatively more accurate in its classification.

SVM model, which can classify patients as either satisfied or dissatisfied patients, helps the hospital to get predictive information about the patient's satisfaction. Hospitals can identify the drawbacks in the service quality dimensions influencing the satisfaction level of the patient. In addition, the study can also be used to compare and benchmark the best hospitals. So we can use these techniques as diagnostic tools to measure the satisfaction levels which in turn help in enhancing the service quality level and the performance levels of the hospital.

© Springer International Publishing AG 2018   67
S. Mohapatra et al., *Service Quality in Indian Hospitals*, Advances in Theory and Practice of Emerging Markets, https://doi.org/10.1007/978-3-319-67888-7_9

9.1.1   Summary and Conclusion

After considering the current service quality scenario in various speciality and multispecialty hospitals, the motivation for this study has aroused specific interest in cardiac care hospitals. It pinned us to work for further research in the area which has not been given the attention it deserves. So the long story cut short, the literature review has been carried out on demographical indices, service quality dimensions and applications of data mining techniques. From the literature review, the gaps and the issues which have to be addressed have been identified. In order to solve the issues, four objectives have been framed. A model has been developed in which ten service quality dimensions will be effecting the patient's satisfaction.

A pre-validated questionnaire having 41 indicators have been identified and used as an instrument for the data collection of the current study. The data has been collected from both the specialty and multispecialty cardiac care hospitals all over India. The first objective considered the demographic variables and clinical quality variables which are eventually influencing the patient's satisfaction. This has been discussed in detail in Chap. 5.

The second objective leads us to develop a SEM model. SEM model is a two-tiered model with a former measurement model and a later structural model. The measurement model constitutes all the 41 indicators influencing the ten service quality dimensions. The structural model consists of all the ten service quality dimensions influencing the patient satisfaction. The data collected has been given as an input for the model using LISREL software. The process is repeated individually for both the specialty and multispecialty cardiac care hospitals. The outputs obtained are analysed and the interpretations are discussed in detail in Chap. 6. The service quality dimensions are prioritized for specialty cardiac care hospitals. The specialty cardiac care hospitals are considered as a benchmark and the multispecialty hospitals are compared with it. The service quality dimensions of multispecialty hospitals have been analysed with the help of rank differences.

The third objective deals with the classification model developed using Artificial Neural Networking. It is explained in detail in Chap. 7. The ANN model is developed for both specialty and multispecialty cardiac care hospitals. The model considers the latent scores obtained from the causal model as the data. The latent scores of all the ten service quality dimensions are taken as the input data and the latent scores of the patient satisfaction are taken as the output data. The number of hidden neurons was calculated based on an empirical formula. The classification model is developed by following a standard structural algorithm in MATLAB. The model stabilizes at some parameters. Here, both the specialty and multispecialty hospitals are compared based on the weights, contributions and spread values. The weights obtained from the study are further analysed to find the lowest contribution, highest contribution and mean contribution values. From this the spread is calculated. The model is validated by using the confusion matrix. The interpretations are discussed in detail based on the study.

The fourth objective deals with the classification model developed by using another data mining technique called support vector machines (SVM). It is dealt in detail in Chap. 8. Here the data will be plotted in space and will be separated by a maximum margin hyperplane. The study considers the latent scores obtained from the causal model as the data for SVMs. SPSS Modeller software is used to analyse the data considered using SVM technique. The model gets stabilized at some parameters. The results are validated using confusion matrices. The confusion matrices obtained by using both the classification techniques are compared in order to find out the best classification technique among both. Likewise the research concentrated on model-based approach in order to analyse and interpret the different facets of service quality influence on patient's satisfaction.

9.2 Conclusion

The proceedings of this study were carried out as discussed in the summary. The conclusions of the study were focussed on the results and discussions of each study. From the demographical study in Chap. 5, it is shown that the clinical variables when compared within the same sort of hospital are insignificant, whereas they are significant when compared with the other sort of hospital. It also concluded that the length of stay of patient in a specialty cardiac care hospital is less, i.e. the patient is cured quickly which results in his satisfaction. In addition the number of visits are portrayed more for specialty cardiac care hospitals. It is also a positive indicator depicting the loyalty of the patients towards specialty cardiac care hospitals.

As pertaining to the study of SEM in Chap. 6, the dimension *communication* gets a high priority in cluster I for specialized cardiac care hospitals. But in the case of multispecialty hospitals it gets least preference status comparatively. The study found the dimensions *responsiveness* and *competence* are important in cluster II for specialized cardiac care hospitals. But in multispecialty hospitals, both these dimensions got the least preference. The implications of this study are that the multispecialty cardiac hospitals can categorize their service delivery by keeping in view the top prioritized dimensions in accordance with the analysis. They can overcome the gaps in service delivery by following the recommendations addressed to them in order to satisfy their patients in every possible aspect.

From the classification study using ANN in Chap. 7, it is concluded that the contribution for satisfaction is more from specialty cardiac care hospitals. As the study proved the significance of weights, the weights obtained are considered to calculate the aggregate score. The maximal aggregate score of specialty cardiac hospitals is more with 8.96 score compared to that of multispecialty hospitals. This projects that the cardiac patients are highly satisfied with specialty cardiac care hospitals. In addition, the classification model has been validated using confusion matrix. The calculated apparent error rate obtained for both specialty and multispecialty hospitals is 4.4% and 11.4%, respectively.

In Chap. 8, for classification model using SVM, the nonlinear classifier has been used with radial basis kernel function. The classification model has been validated by using confusion matrix. The calculated apparent error rate for both specialty and multispecialty hospitals is 3.3% and 9.01%, respectively. It is obvious that the apparent error rate is comparatively less for SVM when compared with that of ANN.

On the whole, the study concludes that the patients of specialty cardiac care are highly satisfied. The clinical quality variables like the length of the stay and the number of visits to the hospital also proved that the specialty cardiac care hospitals are best in satisfying their patients. The SEM model has prioritized the service quality dimensions of specialty cardiac care hospitals influencing the patient satisfaction. So, they can be considered as the benchmark to the multispecialty hospitals. Likewise, the highest contribution of the ANN model proves that the specialty cardiac care patients are highly satisfied when compared with that of multispecialty cardiac care hospitals. In addition, by comparing the obtained apparent error rates from the confusion matrices SVM technique proved to be the best.

Implications of the study include concentrating on the prioritized dimensions which result in patient satisfaction. The classification of the patients into either satisfied or dissatisfied categories helps the hospital to get predictive information about the patient satisfaction. In addition, if any difference occurs in the performance indicators like ALOS (average length of stay), BOR (bed occupancy rate), MR (mortality rate), etc., the reason for change in performance measures can be identified using the predictive and classification models. So we can use these techniques as diagnostic tools to measure the satisfaction levels which in turn help to improve the performance levels of the hospital. As an extension of this research, a new study can be carried out by linking patient satisfaction with loyalty to arrive at loyalty score for the hospitals, and the similar comparative study with respect to other specialities can be carried out as an expansion.

Health care in India has challenges from increasing demand for medical treatments and solutions. Not only the older population needs medical attention but also the younger generation demands higher individual standards for the quality of life. The increase in demand puts a tremendous pressure on administration as well as on nursing staff. Health care has always been the top priority for governments at national level. In line with health-care policies at national level, state governments form their policies so that there can be proper harmony and alignment of policies at all levels. This helps in channelling the available funds in proper direction, thus reducing costs and improving quality through proper standardization of health-care services. Reduction in cost makes availability of health care for all concerned a possibility. However, it requires that a lot of planning is done at all levels for aligning national and regional policies. Hospital management has tried to cope up with this over years, and automation in health management has been used as a strategic tool for addressing the changes in the environment over the last decade. It will be useful to note how this change has evolved with automation. It will also be useful to understand critical success factors involved in this change management process. Different factors such as organization structure, technology infrastructure and implementation approach influence the success of the automation.

With the national emphasis on improving the quality and safety of patient care today, health-care institutions continue to promote new automated systems that will identify and improve organizational performance practices and capabilities. The current operational improvement needs of hospitals and physician group practices need to focus on hospital or group-wide processes, and they should improve the quality of patient care services. Hospital executives desire return from IT infrastructure that can have an immediate effect on operations and costs.

9.3   Limitations and Future Scope of Study

The study was conducted in urban India. The geographical spread and population density in other cities are different. It will be interesting to find business case studies for hospitals in other cities. These practices can be considered as best practices and can be generalized. We could not do this because of difficulties in obtaining data in other cities. In India, it requires a lot of persuasion and convincing to get data from different hospitals. This lack of data from other cities prevented us from making a generalized practice.

The present work can lead to future studies on the role of new technology (viz. cloud computing, internet of things) in health care. With the advent of new technology such as cloud computing and internet of things (IOT), their impact on health care can be explored further. Future studies can also be done on providing affordable health-care solutions by finding effects of different factors, found in this study, on total cost of treatments.

Appendix 1: The Instrument Used for the Study

Questionnaire on Patient Satisfaction

I request you to spend few minutes of your valuable time in filling this questionnaire.

(A) Gender　　Male/Female　　(B) Age:＿＿＿＿＿　　(C) Place:＿＿＿＿

(D) No. of days of stay:＿＿＿＿＿　　(E) No. of visits to the hospital:＿＿＿＿＿

For the statements given below, please rate the extent to which you agree with your hospital (from strongly disagree to strongly agree)

{1, strongly disagree;2, disagree;3, partially disagree;4, neutral;5, partially agree;6, agree;

7, strongly agree}

S. no.	Statements							
1	Cleanliness of the hospital is good	1	2	3	4	5	6	7
2	Pleasantness of the hospital is appealing	1	2	3	4	5	6	7
3	Professional appearance of hospital staff is good	1	2	3	4	5	6	7
4	Professional appearance of other hospital employees is good	1	2	3	4	5	6	7
5	Temperature of the food is sufficient	1	2	3	4	5	6	7
6	Taste of the food is good	1	2	3	4	5	6	7
7	Timing of the meals are accurate	1	2	3	4	5	6	7
8	Physical appearance of your room is appealing	1	2	3	4	5	6	7
9	Availability of visitor parking is convenient	1	2	3	4	5	6	7
10	Availability of information about your condition is up to date	1	2	3	4	5	6	7
11	Ease of getting hold of hospital personnel on the phone is good	1	2	3	4	5	6	7
12	Availability of meals for the family is convenient	1	2	3	4	5	6	7

(continued)

© Springer International Publishing AG 2018

S. Mohapatra et al., *Service Quality in Indian Hospitals*, Advances in Theory and Practice of Emerging Markets, https://doi.org/10.1007/978-3-319-67888-7

S. no.	Statements							
13	Availability of sleeping accommodations for your family is convenient	1	2	3	4	5	6	7
14	Concern for family and visitors is good	1	2	3	4	5	6	7
15	Concern for your particular needs is good	1	2	3	4	5	6	7
16	Amount of time spent by staff getting to know and understand your needs is sufficient	1	2	3	4	5	6	7
17	Politeness of physicians is good	1	2	3	4	5	6	7
18	Politeness of the nurses is good	1	2	3	4	5	6	7
19	Politeness of other hospital staff is good	1	2	3	4	5	6	7
20	Performance of services when they were supposed to be performed is good	1	2	3	4	5	6	7
21	Performance of services in the way you were told they would be performed is up to your expectation	1	2	3	4	5	6	7
22	Sense of security from physical harm that you felt in the hospital is good	1	2	3	4	5	6	7
23	Sense of well-being you felt in the hospital is good	1	2	3	4	5	6	7
24	Ability of the hospital to deliver what was promised in their advertising	1	2	3	4	5	6	7
25	Ability of the hospital to treat you the way you expected to be treated	1	2	3	4	5	6	7
26	Responsiveness of the nurses to your needs is good	1	2	3	4	5	6	7
27	Responsiveness of the physicians to your needs is good	1	2	3	4	5	6	7
28	Waiting time for tests is low	1	2	3	4	5	6	7
29	Speed and ease of admissions is fast	1	2	3	4	5	6	7
30	Speed and ease of discharge is fast	1	2	3	4	5	6	7
31	Waiting time for refund (if due) is less	1	2	3	4	5	6	7
32	Waiting time for medication is less	1	2	3	4	5	6	7
33	Time between admission and getting in your room is low	1	2	3	4	5	6	7
34	Adequacy of instructions given at time of release on how to care for yourself	1	2	3	4	5	6	7
35	Adequacy of explanation about your condition and treatment by hospital staff	1	2	3	4	5	6	7
36	Instructions about billing procedures are given	1	2	3	4	5	6	7
37	Skill of the nurses attending you is good	1	2	3	4	5	6	7
38	Skill of the physicians attending you is good	1	2	3	4	5	6	7
39	Skill of those who performed the test is good	1	2	3	4	5	6	7
40	Accuracy of the billing procedure is fine	1	2	3	4	5	6	7
41	Competence of the staff in filing insurance claims is good	1	2	3	4	5	6	7

Appendix 2: The Macro View of the Structural Equational Model

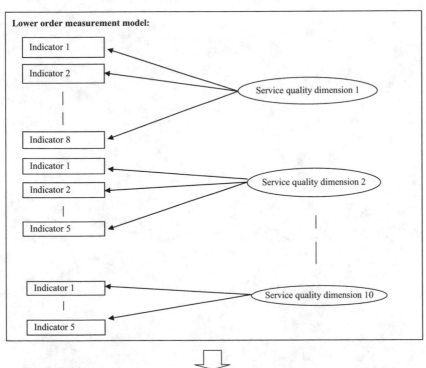

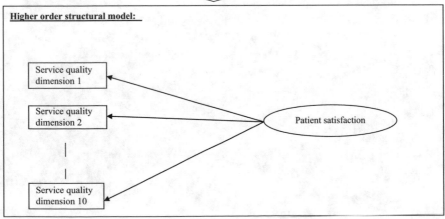

© Springer International Publishing AG 2018
S. Mohapatra et al., *Service Quality in Indian Hospitals*, Advances in Theory and
Practice of Emerging Markets, https://doi.org/10.1007/978-3-319-67888-7

Appendix 3: The Proposed Measurement Model for Cardiac Patient's Satisfaction

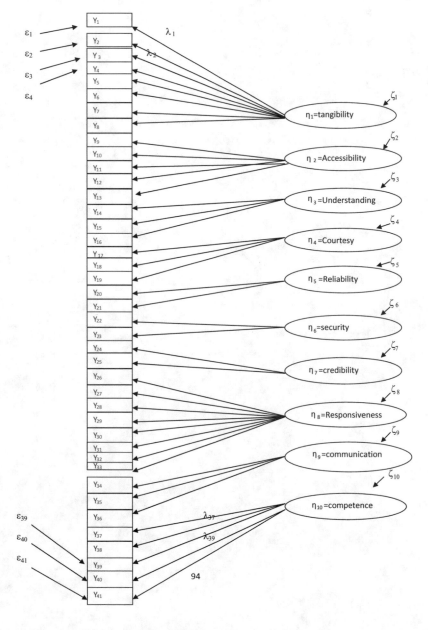

Appendix 4: The Proposed Structural Model for Cardiac Patient's Satisfaction

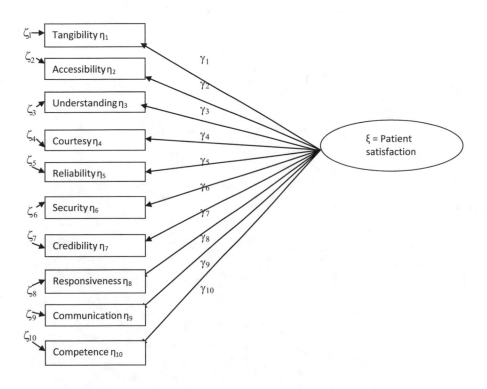

S. Mohapatra et al., *Service Quality in Indian Hospitals*, Advances in Theory and Practice of Emerging Markets, https://doi.org/10.1007/978-3-319-67888-7

Appendix 5: Hypobook Depicting the 41 Indicators Representing the Ten Dimensions of Service Quality

Dimension			Hypobook
Tangibility (Tn)	Tn_1	Y_1	Cleanliness of the hospital influences tangibility
	Tn_2	Y_2	Pleasantness of the hospital influences tangibility
	Tn_3	Y_3	Professional appearance of hospital staff influences tangibility
	Tn_4	Y_4	Professional appearance of other hospital employees influences tangibility
	Tn_5	Y_5	Temperature of the food influences tangibility
	Tn_6	Y_6	Taste of the food influences tangibility
	Tn_7	Y_7	Timing of the meals influences tangibility
	Tn_8	Y_8	Physical appearance of the room influences tangibility
Accessibility (Ac)	Ac_1	Y_9	Availability of visitor parking influences accessibility
	Ac_2	Y_{10}	Availability of information about patient condition is up to date influences accessibility
	Ac_3	Y_{11}	Ease of getting hold of hospital personnel on the phone influences accessibility
	Ac_4	Y_{12}	Availability of meals for the family influences accessibility
	Ac_5	Y_{13}	Availability of sleeping accommodations for the family influences accessibility
Understanding (Un)	Un_1	Y_{14}	Concern for family and visitors influences understanding
	Un_2	Y_{15}	Concern for your particular needs influences understanding
	Un_3	Y_{16}	Amount of time spent by staff getting to know and understand your needs influences understanding
Courtesy (Cu)	Cu_1	Y_{17}	Politeness of physicians influences courtesy
	Cu_2	Y_{18}	Politeness of the nurses influences courtesy
	Cu_3	Y_{19}	Politeness of other hospital staff influences courtesy

(continued)

© Springer International Publishing AG 2018
S. Mohapatra et al., *Service Quality in Indian Hospitals*, Advances in Theory and Practice of Emerging Markets, https://doi.org/10.1007/978-3-319-67888-7

Dimension			Hypobook
Reliability (Rl)	Rl_1	Y_{20}	Performance of services when they were supposed to be performed influences reliability
	Rl_2	Y_{21}	Performance of services in the way you were told they would be performed influences reliability
Secure (Se)	Se_1	Y_{22}	Sense of security from physical harm that you felt in the hospital influences security
	Se_2	Y_{23}	Sense of well-being you felt in the hospital influences security
Credibility (Cr)	Cr_1	Y_{24}	Ability of the hospital to deliver what was promised in their advertising influences credibility
	Cr_2	Y_{25}	Ability of the hospital to treat you the way you expected to be treated influences credibility
Responsiveness (Rs)	Rs_1	Y_{26}	Response of the nurses to your needs influences responsiveness
	Rs_2	Y_{27}	Response of the physicians to your needs influences responsiveness
	Rs_3	Y_{28}	Waiting time for tests influences responsiveness
	Rs_4	Y_{29}	Speed and ease of admissions influences responsiveness
	Rs_5	Y_{30}	Speed and ease of discharge influences responsiveness
	Rs_6	Y_{31}	Waiting time for refund (if due) influences responsiveness
	Rs_7	Y_{32}	Waiting time for medication influences responsiveness
	Rs_8	Y_{33}	Time between admission and getting in your room influences responsiveness
Communication (Cm)	Cm_1	Y_{34}	Adequacy of instructions given at time of release on how to care for yourself influences communication
	Cm_2	Y_{35}	Adequacy of explanation about your condition and treatment by hospital staff influences communication
	Cm_3	Y_{36}	Instructions about billing procedures influence communication
Competence (Cp)	Cp_1	Y_{37}	Skill of the nurses attending you influences competence
	Cp_2	Y_{38}	Skill of the physicians attending you influences competence
	Cp_3	Y_{39}	Skill of those who performed the test influences competence
	Cp_4	Y_{40}	Accuracy of the billing procedure influences competence
	Cp_5	Y_{41}	Competence of the staff in filing insurance claims influences competence

Appendix 6: Estimates of Measurement Model for Speciality Cardiac Care Hospitals

Variable	Point estimate	*t*-value
Tangibility (n1)		
Cleanliness of the hospital is good (y1)	0.017	12.23
Pleasantness of the hospital is appealing (y2)	−0.089	12.21
Professional appearance of hospital staff is good (y3)	0.062	12.22
Professional appearance of other hospital employees is good (y4)	−0.039	12.22
Temperature of the food is sufficient (y5)	−1.10	10.88
Taste of the food is good (y6)	−0.85	11.86
Timing of the meals is accurate (y7)	−1.39	6.41
Physical appearance of your room is appealing (y8)	−0.012	12.23
Accessibility (n2)		
Availability of visitor parking is convenient (y9)	0.97	11.8
Availability of information about your condition is up to date (y10)	0.17	12.17
Ease of getting hold of hospital personnel on the phone is good (y11)	0.072	12.22
Availability of meals for the family is convenient (y12)	1.43	7.68
Availability of sleeping accommodations for your family is convenient (y13)	1.45	9.46
Understanding (n3)		
Concern for family and visitors is good (y14)	1.37	8.1
Concern for your particular needs is good (y15)	−0.0036	12.23
Amount of time spent by staff getting to know and understand your needs is sufficient (y16)	−0.072	12.21
Courtesy (n4)		
Politeness of physicians is good (y17)	0.48	6.56
Politeness of the nurses is good (y18)	0.33	9.86

(continued)

S. Mohapatra et al., *Service Quality in Indian Hospitals*, Advances in Theory and Practice of Emerging Markets, https://doi.org/10.1007/978-3-319-67888-7

Variable	Point estimate	t-value
Politeness of other hospital staff is good (y19)	0.25	11.29
Reliability (n5)		
Performance of services when they were supposed to be performed is good (y20)	0.48	2.8
Performance of services in the way you were told they would be performed is up to your expectation (y21)	0.49	2.85
Security (n6)		
Sense of security from physical harm that you felt in the hospital is good (y22)	0.097	11.71
Sense of well-being you felt in the hospital is good (y23)	0.21	6.79
Credibility (n7)		
Ability of the hospital to deliver what was promised in their advertising (y24)	0.26	9.65
Ability of the hospital to treat you the way you expected to be treated (y25)	0.3	5.98
Responsiveness (n8)		
Responsiveness of the nurses to your needs is good (y26)	−0.07	12.18
Responsiveness of the physicians to your needs is good (y27)	0.039	12.21
Waiting time for tests is less (y28)	0.66	9.92
Speed and ease of admissions is fast (y29)	0.024	12.22
Speed and ease of discharge is fast (y30)	0.82	9.51
Waiting time for refund (if due) is less (y31)	0.65	9.12
Waiting time for medication is less (y32)	0.69	10.77
Time between admission and getting in your room is less (y33)	0.11	11.99
Communication (n9)		
Adequacy of instructions given at time of discharge on how to care for yourself (y34)	0.084	11.15
Adequacy of explanation about your condition and treatment by hospital staff (y35)	0.0076	12.23
Instructions about billing procedures are given (y36)	0.28	8.5
Competence (n10)		
Skill of the nurses attending you is good (y37)	0.4	10.55
Skill of the physicians attending you is good (y38)	0.52	8.64
Skill of those who performed the test is good (y39)	0.43	9.4
Accuracy of the billing procedure is good (y40)	0.44	11.89
Competence of the staff in filing insurance claims is good (y41)	0.18	12.17

Appendix 7: Estimates of Measurement Model for Multispecialty Hospitals

Variable	Point estimate	t-value
Tangibility (n1)		
Cleanliness of the hospital is good (y1)	0.34	13.71
Pleasantness of the hospital is appealing (y2)	0.15	13.89
Professional appearance of hospital staff is good (y3)	−0.017	14.21
Professional appearance of other hospital employees is good (y4)	−0.0012	14.21
Temperature of the food is sufficient (y5)	0.89	10.67
Taste of the food is good (y6)	0.72	12.23
Timing of the meals is accurate (y7)	1.17	7.17
Physical appearance of your room is appealing (y8)	0.2	13.94
Accessibility (n2)		
Availability of visitor parking is convenient (y9)	0.48	14
Availability of information about your condition is up to date (y10)	0.12	14.14
Ease of getting hold of hospital personnel on the phone is good (y11)	−0.097	14.18
Availability of meals for the family is convenient (y12)	1.2	9.27
Availability of sleeping accommodations for your family is convenient (y13)	1.28	7.29
Understanding (n3)		
Concern for family and visitors is good (y14)	0.83	7.81
Concern for your particular needs is good (y15)	−0.03	14.24
Amount of time spent by staff getting to know and understand your needs is sufficient (y16)	−0.16	13.84
Courtesy (n4)		
Politeness of physicians is good (y17)	0.10	14.03
Politeness of the nurses is good (y18)	0.53	3.14
Politeness of other hospital staff is good (y19)	0.35	12.3

(continued)

© Springer International Publishing AG 2018
S. Mohapatra et al., *Service Quality in Indian Hospitals*, Advances in Theory and
Practice of Emerging Markets, https://doi.org/10.1007/978-3-319-67888-7

Variable	Point estimate	t-value
Reliability (n5)		
Performance of services when they were supposed to be performed is good (y20)	0.62	3.21
Performance of services in the way you were told they would be performed is up to your expectation (y21)	0.5	6.68
Security (n6)		
Sense of security from physical harm that you felt in the hospital is good (y22)	0.16	8.08
Sense of well-being you felt in the hospital is good (y23)	0.074	13.48
Credibility (n7)		
Ability of the hospital to deliver what was promised in their advertising (y24)	0.19	8.04
Ability of the hospital to treat you the way you expected to be treated (y25)	0.15	10.32
Responsiveness (n8)		
Responsiveness of the nurses to your needs is good (y26)	0.4	10.12
Responsiveness of the physicians to your needs is good (y27)	0.09	14.11
Waiting time for tests is less (y28)	−0.24	14.12
Speed and ease of admissions is fast (y29)	0.038	14.2
Speed and ease of discharge is fast (y30)	−0.5	13.54
Waiting time for refund (if due) is less (y31)	−0.2	14.12
Waiting time for medication is less (y32)	0.13	14.2
Time between admission and getting in your room is less (y33)	0.031	14.21
Communication (n9)		
Adequacy of instructions given at time of release on how to care for yourself (y34)	0.17	12.45
Adequacy of explanation about your condition and treatment by hospital staff (y35)	0.24	9.69
Instructions about billing procedures are given (y36)	0.066	14.19
Competence (n10)		
Skill of the nurses attending you is good (y37)	0.44	10.41
Skill of the physicians attending you is good (y38)	0.11	14.14
Skill of those who performed the test is good (y39)	0.23	13.73
Accuracy of the billing procedure is good (y40)	−0.24	14.17
Competence of the staff in filing insurance claims is good (y41)	−0.52	13.68

Appendix 8

(a) *Measurement model of speciality cardiac care hospitals*

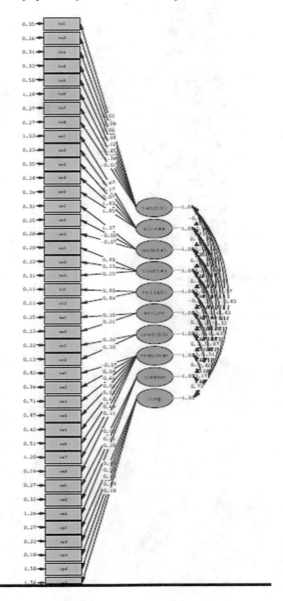

© Springer International Publishing AG 2018
S. Mohapatra et al., *Service Quality in Indian Hospitals*, Advances in Theory and
Practice of Emerging Markets, https://doi.org/10.1007/978-3-319-67888-7

(b)*Structural model of speciality cardiac care hospitals*

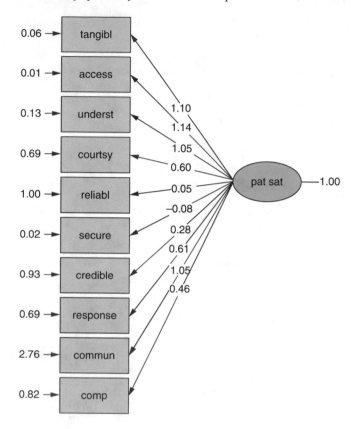

(c) *Measurement model of multispecialty hospitals*

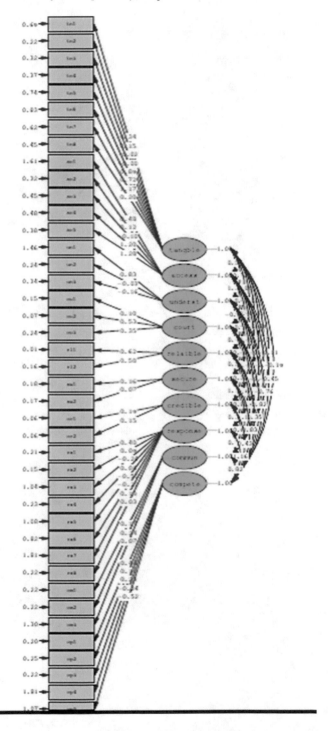

(d)*Structural model for multispecialty hospitals*

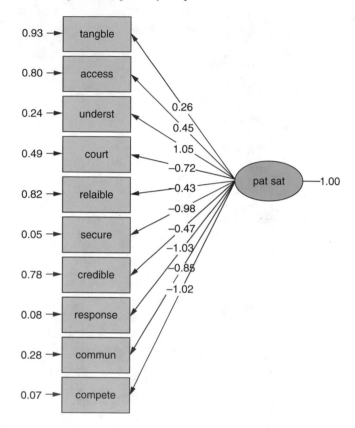

Appendix 9: Weights of Input to Hidden Layer in Specialty Cardiac Care Hospitals

Hidden neuron	Tang (L1)	Acces (L2)	Undr (L3)	Cour (L4)	Relia (L5)	Sec (L6)	Cred (L7)	Resp (L8)	Comm (L9)	Comp (L10)
Y1	0.29	−0.09	0.32	0.98	−0.94	0.51	−0.07	0.82	−0.04	−0.88
Y2	0.68	−0.08	0.29	1.07	−0.42	−0.34	0.59	0.25	−0.92	−0.38
Y3	0.34	−0.15	−0.74	−0.19	0.79	−0.31	0.48	−0.71	0.75	0.72
Y4	−0.25	−0.55	−0.31	−0.55	−0.71	0.86	0.41	0.006	0.47	0.44
Y5	0.06	0.34	−0.09	−0.24	0.59	−0.76	0.75	0.49	0.37	−0.63
Y6	−0.58	0.13	−0.26	−0.34	0.072	0.71	−0.18	−1.27	−0.44	−0.15
Y7	0.14	0.52	0.34	−0.12	0.11	0.89	0.46	−0.41	−0.11	−0.33
Y8	−0.78	0.41	−0.71	−0.41	0.18	0.53	−0.65	−0.63	0.17	−0.35
Y9	0.14	0.62	−0.76	−0.09	−0.11	−0.58	−0.18	0.27	0.26	0.06
Y10	0.08	−0.74	−0.31	−0.01	0.03	−0.26	0.07	0.11	0.07	−0.04
Y11	−0.39	0.42	−0.62	−0.67	1.14	−0.35	−0.13	−0.04	0.63	−0.68
Y12	0.64	0.31	−0.17	−1.44	0.06	0.71	0.008	−0.17	−0.19	−0.09
Y13	0.53	−0.32	−0.28	−0.29	−0.12	−0.75	0.91	−1.006	−0.104	−0.75
Y14	0.22	1.38	0.27	−0.01	−0.08	0.09	0.02	0.06	0.011	0.09
Y15	0.68	1.64	−0.02	0.06	−0.01	−0.23	0.15	0.04	−0.01	−0.02
Y16	0.46	−0.003	−0.92	0.12	0.13	0.24	0.61	−1.06	−0.66	−0.89

© Springer International Publishing AG 2018
S. Mohapatra et al., *Service Quality in Indian Hospitals*, Advances in Theory and Practice of Emerging Markets, https://doi.org/10.1007/978-3-319-67888-7

Appendix 10: Weights of Hidden Layer to Output in Speciality Cardiac Care Hospitals

Hidden neurons	Output neuron (z)
Y1	−0.013
Y2	0.016
Y3	0.02
Y4	−0.04
Y5	0.02
Y6	0.05
Y7	0.11
Y8	−0.12
Y9	0.31
Y10	−0.7
Y11	0.01
Y12	−0.006
Y13	−0.03
Y14	1.27
Y15	1.19
Y16	0.04

© Springer International Publishing AG 2018
S. Mohapatra et al., *Service Quality in Indian Hospitals*, Advances in Theory and Practice of Emerging Markets, https://doi.org/10.1007/978-3-319-67888-7

Appendix 11: Weights of Input to Hidden Layer in Multispecialty Cardiac Care Hospitals

Hidden neuron	Tang (L1)	Acces (L2)	Undr (L3)	Cour (L4)	Relia (L5)	Sec (L6)	Cred (L7)	Resp (L8)	Commu (L9)	Comp (L10)
Y1	0.71	−0.17	−0.56	0.41	0.8826	−0.3369	0.23	−0.62	−0.57	−0.17
Y2	0.33	0.52	−0.81	0.37	0.57	0.74	−0.14	0.69	0.33	−0.36
Y3	−0.65	0.38	−0.53	−0.36	−0.11	0.03	−0.77	−0.73	−0.07	−0.64
Y4	0.66	0.84	0.67	0.2	−0.65	0.03	−0.31	0.52	0.58	−0.64
Y5	0.25	0.47	0.51	0.29	−0.64	0.77	−0.82	−0.11	−0.86	−0.85
Y6	−0.6	−0.71	−0.08	−0.68	−0.49	−0.65	0.51	0.62	−0.57	−0.78
Y7	0.02	0.41	0.54	−0.63	−0.05	0.66	0.08	−0.27	−0.19	0.016
Y8	0.15	0.76	−1.13	0.11	−0.52	0.76	0.21	0.24	−0.44	−0.59
Y9	0.79	0.18	−0.16	0.79	0.51	−0.13	−0.57	−0.59	0.63	0.69
Y10	0.03	0.1	−0.04	−0.03	0.01	−0.08	0.001	0.51	−0.006	0.62
Y11	0.15	0.17	0.39	0.21	0.05	−0.61	−0.07	−0.49	0.17	−0.41
Y12	0.5	−0.19	0.19	−0.22	−0.38	−0.56	0.76	0.77	−0.11	0.16
Y13	0.91	0.37	−0.71	0.43	−0.67	0.12	0.4	0.76	0.85	−0.32
Y14	−0.18	−0.14	−0.22	−0.21	−0.07	0.56	0.07	0.35	−0.24	0.58
Y15	−0.04	−0.09	0.39	0.03	0.08	0.37	0.05	−1.15	−0.09	−0.79
Y16	−0.73	−0.99	0.3	0.36	0.15	−0.83	−0.97	−0.4	−0.14	−0.95

© Springer International Publishing AG 2018
S. Mohapatra et al., *Service Quality in Indian Hospitals*, Advances in Theory and Practice of Emerging Markets, https://doi.org/10.1007/978-3-319-67888-7

Appendix 12: The Weights of Hidden Layer to Output in Multispecialty Hospitals

Hidden neurons	Output neuron (z)
Y1	−0.009
Y2	0.013
Y3	−0.057
Y4	0.017
Y5	0.008
Y6	−0.016
Y7	−0.217
Y8	−0.0108
Y9	0.0174
Y10	1.0772
Y11	−1.0125
Y12	−0.0743
Y13	0.0310
Y14	0.2870
Y15	−1.1878
Y16	0.0140

© Springer International Publishing AG 2018
S. Mohapatra et al., *Service Quality in Indian Hospitals*, Advances in Theory and Practice of Emerging Markets, https://doi.org/10.1007/978-3-319-67888-7

Appendix 13: Neural Network Model

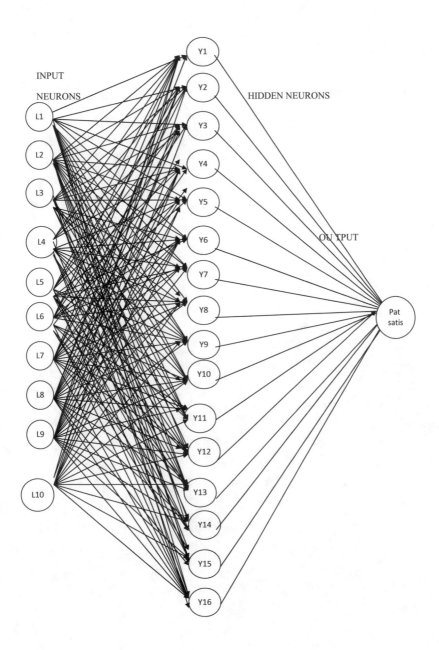

References

Aagja JP, Garg R (2010) Measuring perceived service quality for public hospitals(PubHosQual) in the Indian context. Int J Pharm Healthc Mark 4(1):60–83

Alanis AY, Leon BS, Sanchez EN, Ruiz-Velazquez E (2011) Blood glucose level neural model for type 1 diabetes mellitus patients. Int J Neural Syst 21(6):491–504

Alrubaiee L, Alkaa'ida F (2011) The mediating effect of patient satisfaction in the patients' perceptions of healthcare quality – patient trust relationship. Int J Mark Stud 3(1):103–127

Al-salim B (2008) Mass customization of travel packages: data mining approach. Int J Flex Manuf Syst 19:612–624

Arasli H, Haktan Ekiz E, Turan Katircioglu S (2008) Gearing service quality into public and private hospitals in small islands-empirical evidence from Cyprus. Int J Health Care Qual Assur 21(1):8–23

Ariffin AAM, Aziz NA (2008) Determining the service quality dimensions and zone of tolerance for hospital services in Malaysia. Bus Rev, Cambridge 10(2):164–169

Babakus E, Mangold WG (1992) Adapting the SERVQUAL scale to hospital services: an empirical investigation. Health Serv Res 26(6):767–786

Bahia K, Nantel J (2000) A reliable and valid measurement scale for the perceived service quality of banks. Int J Bank Mark 18(2):84–91

Baxter L (2004) Up to scratch? Occup Health 56(3):24

Burges CJC (1998) A tutorial on support vector machines for pattern recognition. Data Min Knowl Disc 2(2):121–167

Buttle F (1996) SERVQUAL: review, critique, research agenda. Eur J Mark 30(1):8–32

Chowdhury MMU (2008) Customer expectations and management perceptions in healthcare services of Bangladesh: an overview. J Serv Res 8(2):121–140

Dabholkar PA, Thorpe DI, Rentz JO (1996) A measure of service quality for retail stores: scale development and validation. J Acad Mark Sci 24(1):3–16

Dean AM (1999) The applicability of SERVQUAL in different health care environments. Health Mark Q 16(3):1–15

Eakuru N, Mat NKN (2008) The application of structural equation modeling (SEM) in determining the antecedents of customer loyalty in banks in South Thailand. Bus Rev (Cambridge) 10(2):782–800

Elleuch A (2008) Patient satisfaction in Japan. Int J Health Care Qual Assur 21(7):692–705

© Springer International Publishing AG 2018

S. Mohapatra et al., *Service Quality in Indian Hospitals*, Advances in Theory and Practice of Emerging Markets, https://doi.org/10.1007/978-3-319-67888-7

Ericreidenbach R, Smallwood BS (1990) Exploring perceptions of hospital operations by a modified SERVQUAL approach. J Health Care Mark 10(4):47–55

Golmohammadi A, Shams Ghareneh N, Keramati AA, Jahandideh B (2011) Importance analysis of travel attributes using a rough set-based neural network. The case of Iranian tourism industry. J Hosp Tour Technol 2(2):155–171

Hsu K-P, Hsieh S-H, Hsieh S-L, Cheng P-H, Weng Y-C, Wu J-H, Lai F (2010) A newborn screening system based on service-oriented architecture embedded support vector machine. J Med Syst 34:899–907

Jabnoun N, Al Rasasi AJ (2005) Transformational leadership and service quality in UAE hospitals. Manag Serv Qual 15(1):70–81

de Jager J, du Plooy T (2011) Are public hospitals responding to tangible and reliable service-related needs of patients in the new South Africa? J Manag Policy Pract 12(2):103

Khashman A (2008) Blood cell identification using a simple neural network. Int J Neural Syst 18(5):453–458

Kilbourne WE, Duff JA, Duffy M, Giarchi G (2004) The applicability of SERVQUAL in cross-national measurements of healthcare quality. J Serv Mark 18(7):524–533

Lam SSK (1997) Servqual; a tool for measuring patients' opinions of hospital service quality in Hongkong. Total Qual Manag 8(4):145–152

Lee W-I, Shih B-Y (2007) Application of neural networks to recognize profitable customers for dental services marketing-a case of dental clinics in Taiwan. Expert Syst Appl 36:199–208

Li J, Huang K-Y, Jin J, Shi J (2007) A survey on statistical methods for health care fraud detection. Health Care Manag Sci 11:275–287

Mostafa MM (2005) An empirical study of patients' expectations and satisfactions in Egyptian hospitals. Int J Health Care Qual Assur 18(7):516–532

Owusu-Frimpong N, Nwankwo S (2010) Measuring service quality and patient satisfaction with access to public and private healthcare delivery. Int J Public Sect Manag 23(3):203–220

Pakdil F, Harwood TN (2005) Patient satisfaction in a preoperative assessment clinic: an analysis using SERVQUAL dimensions. Total Qual Manag 16(1):15–30

Parasuraman A, Zeithaml VA, Berry LL (1985) A conceptual model of service quality and its implications for future research. J Mark 49:41–50

Parasuraman A, Zeithaml VA, Berry LL (1988) SERVQUAL: a multiple-item scale for measuring consumer perceptions of service quality. J Retail 64(1):12–40

Patil BM, Joshi RC, Toshniwal D, Biradar S (2011) A new approach: role of data mining in prediction of survival of burn patients. J Med Syst 35:1531–1542

Rohini R, Mahadevappa B (2006) Service quality in Bangalore hospitals –an empirical study. J Serv Res 6(1):59–83

Rosenthal SL, Biro FM, Succop PA, Berstein DL, Stanberry LR (1997) Impact of demographics, sexual history, and psychological functioning on the acquisition of STDs in adolescents. Adolescence; Winter 32(128):757–769

Roshnee Ramsaran-Fowdar R (2008) The relative importance of service dimensions in a healthcare setting. Int J Health Care Qual Assur 21(1):104–124

Schnoll RA, Harlow LL (2001) Using disease-related and demographic variables to form cancer-distress risk groups. J Behav Med 24(1):57–74

Schwartz C, Frohner R (2005) Contribution of demographic, medical, and social support variables in predicting the mental health dimension of quality of life among people with multiple sclerosis. Health Soc Work 30(3):203–212

Su C-T, Wang P-C, Chen Y-C, Chen L-F (2012) Data mining techniques for assisting the diagnosis of pressure ulcer development in surgical patients. J Med Syst 36:2387–2399

Taner T, Antony J (2006) Comparing public and private hospital care service quality in Turkey. Leadersh Health Serv 19(2):1–10

Vandamme R, Leunis J (1993) Development of a multiple-item scale for measuring hospital service quality. Int J Serv Ind Manag 4(3):30–49

Vapnik V (1998) Statistical learning theory. Springer, New York

Viveros MS, Nearhos JP, Rothman MJ (1996) Applyong data mining techniques to a health insurance information system: Proceedings of the 22nd VLDB conference, India

Wahl A, Moum T, Hanestad BR, Wiklund I (1999) The relationship between demographic and clinical variables, and quality of life aspects in patients with psoriasis. Qual Life Res 8:319–326

Wang M-Y (2007) Measuring e-CRM service quality in the library context:a preliminary study. Electron Libr 26(6):896–911

Wang Y, Huang L (2009) Risk assessment of supply chain based on BP neural network. Second international symposium on knowledge acquisition and modeling, New York

Wicks AM, Chin WW (2008) Measuring the three process segments of a customer's service experience for an out-patient surgery center. Int J Health Care Qual Assur 21(1):24–38

Wisniewski M, Wisniewski H (2005) Measuring service quality in a hospital colonoscopy clinic. Int J Health Care Qual Assur 18(2/3):217–228

Yaacob MA, Zakaria Z, Salamat ASA, Yaacob Z, Salmi NA, Hasan NF, Razak R, Nafisah S, Rahim A (2011) Patients satisfaction towards service quality in public hospital: Malaysia perspective. Interdiscip J Contemp Res Bus 2(12):635

Youssef F, Nel D, Bovaird T (1995) Service quality in NHS hospitals. J Manag Med 9(1):66–74

Web References [Accessed on and Before 20th December 2011]

Web link 1. http://www.moneycontrol.com/smementor/news/indian-markets/healthcare-sector-likely-to-hit-155bn-revenue-by-2017-792867.html

Web link 2. https://en.wikipedia.org/wiki/Hospital

Web link 3. https://books.google.com/. Risse GB (1990) Mending bodies, saving souls: a history of hospitals. Oxford University Press

Web link 4. https://books.google.com/. Roderick E McGrew, Encyclopaedia of medical history (Macmillan 1985)

Web link 5. https://en.wikipedia.org/wiki/Clinics

Web link 6. http://www.pwc.com/gx/healthcare/pdf/emerging-market-report-hc-in-india.pdf

Web link 7. http://healthcare.financialexpress.com/201101/anniversaryspecial09.shtml

Web link 8. http://articles.timesofindia.indiatimes.com/2011-10-16/mumbai/30285785_1_oncology-services-cardiac-care-maternity-services

Web link 9. http://www.world-heart.org/doc/10764

Web link 10. http://info@medicaltourismworld.in

Index

© Springer International Publishing AG 2018   105
S. Mohapatra et al., *Service Quality in Indian Hospitals*, Advances in Theory and
Practice of Emerging Markets, https://doi.org/10.1007/978-3-319-67888-7

Printed in the United States
By Bookmasters